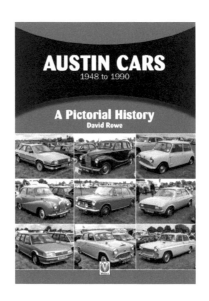

AUSTIN CARS
1948 to 1990

A Pictorial History
David Rowe

T0386707

VELOCE PUBLISHING
THE PUBLISHER OF FINE AUTOMOTIVE BOOKS

First published in November 2018, reprinted April 2021 by Veloce Publishing Limited, Veloce House, Parkway Farm Business Park, Middle Farm Way, Poundbury, Dorchester DT1 3AR, England.
Tel +44 (0)1305 260068 / Fax 01305 250479 / e-mail info@veloce.co.uk / web www.veloce.co.uk or www.velocebooks.com. ISBN: 978-1-787112-19-3 UPC: 6-36847-01219-9.

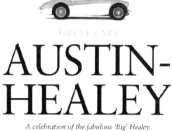

INDEX

AUSTIN CARS
1948 to 1990

A Pictorial History
David Rowe

CONTENTS

For full model listing, see the Index

A history of Austin

Herbert Austin was born in 1866 in Yorkshire, and moved to Australia in 1884, where he worked for a number of engineering firms before joining the Wolseley Sheep-Shearing Machine Company. Whilst there, he was able to demonstrate his abilities, and improve the equipment. Having taken out patents on the changes he made, he was given shares in the company, and was appointed manager of the company's Birmingham-based English branch. Eventually, Austin found himself reliant on sub-contractors whose products were often defective, and so, recognising that a growing number of cycle manufacturers – such as Humber, Rover, and Singer – were beginning to appear around Birmingham, he decided to turn his attention to manufacturing parts for these companies, and ultimately became an agent, selling their cycles. Following a visit to Paris in 1895, he became interested in a Bollée motor tricycle, and upon his return to England built his own version of this car. He subsequently persuaded the directors of the Wolseley company to provide money to build a second three-wheeler for display at the National Cycle Exhibition at Crystal Palace. The public, however, were more interested in the four-wheeled motor cars that were beginning to appear, and so Austin produced a four-wheeler. He drove this car in the 1000-mile trial organised by the Automobile Club of Great Britain in 1900, which he successfully completed. The car had tiller steering and a combination of belt and chain drives; later cars were to be equipped with wheeled steering and had chain drive only.

Austin then decided that the Wolseley company should start producing motor cars in quantity. However, the company was unable to provide sufficient financial support to Austin, so he turned to Sir Hiram Maxim, a man whom Austin had previously met, and who had expressed an interest in producing motor cars. Maxim's company had been acquired by Vickers, which also owned The Barrow Shipbuilding Company, and although it was interested in the idea of producing cars, it did not agree with Austin's ideas of using horizontally-opposed engines, whilst other manufacturers were turning to vertical engines.

How ironic that one of the most successful cars of all time, the Volkswagen Beetle, first developed some thirty years later, used a horizontally-opposed engine. The Wolseley Sheep-Shearing Machine Company was soon divided into two separate companies: one to continue the original business, and the other to produce motor cars at Adderley Park in Birmingham. However, with the public turning to vertically-engined cars, sales of Wolseleys fell, and Austin left the company in 1905. With the support of the Du Cros family, owners of the Dunlop tyre company, he set up his own business – The Austin Motor Company – on the site of a disused printing works at Longbridge, near Birmingham.

The first Austin car to be built, a 25/30hp model launched in 1906, was a success, so in order to gain publicity for his new business, Austin produced three cars specifically for the 1908 French Grand Prix. Cars of various hp ratings were produced up until 1913, with a night shift being introduced at the factory in 1910 in order to satisfy demand. In 1913, Austin decided to enter the heavy commercial market, before pulling out again shortly after.

Austin's cars featured a range of different body styles, from open top landaulet to fully enclosed limousine, with the most popular model being a 20hp known as the Twenty. During the period from 1914 to 1918, as well as the Twenty, the Longbridge plant produced munitions, armoured cars, ambulances, lorries and aeroplanes.

From 1919, Austin decided to concentrate solely on the Twenty. However, as the Great Depression approached, this reliance on what was, at the time, considered to be a large car, ultimately led to the company being placed in receivership, a fate some other companies would also experience. In 1922, a scaled down Twenty – the Twelve – was introduced, and this car continued in production until the 1930s. The Austin Seven, designed by Stanley Edge and fitted with a 750cc engine, is one model for which the Austin Motor Company is still remembered. Introduced in 1923, it went on to be built under licence by BMW in Germany and Datsun (Nissan) in Japan. Reliant even used a version of this engine in its three-wheelers from 1937 until 1962, by which time a totally different Seven had appeared on the scenes: the 1959 Mini!

The original Seven continued in production until 1939, when it was replaced by the Eight. This car had a completely different body style. Gone was the boxy shape, replaced by a curved, more aerodynamic body style, which now featured across the whole range of Austin cars.

In 1936, Austin became chairman of the Government's shadow factory scheme, with manufacturers building additional factories to produce munitions, motor vehicles, and aeroplanes. Following the cessation of the war in 1945, production of Austin motor cars recommenced. These were versions of the 1939 models – the Eight, Ten, Twelve, and Sixteen.

In 1946, the millionth Austin car, a Sixteen, was produced. It was signed by all the workers and is now on display at the British Motor Industry Heritage Centre at Gaydon. With the Government desperate to cover the debts it had incurred during the war, manufacturers were pressed to export, with North America seen as a key market. The first of the new postwar-designed cars (the 'Counties' models, the Devon and Dorset) were sent there, followed shortly by the rather appropriately named Atlantic model. Further cars named after British counties appeared between 1948 and 1954, with the Cambridge name continuing to be used until 1969.

In 1952, the Austin Motor Company merged with the Nuffield Organisation to become BMC (British Motor Corporation).

Herbert Austin died in 1941, the business having been run since 1938 by Leonard Lord, who had previously been responsible for the Wolseley Car Company, which had been acquired by the Nuffield Organisation in 1927. Other companies owned by Nuffield included Morris, MG and Riley. In 1959, with the arrival of the Farina-designed cars, the Austin Cambridge, Morris Oxford, MG Magnette, Riley 4/68, and Wolseley 15/60, which all used the same bodyshell, the Austin and Wolseley names became synonymous, with Wolseley cars being upmarket versions of the Austin models. Generally, after 1959, BMC began 'badge engineering,' a practice adopted by many other manufacturers, such as the Rootes

Group, whose Singer cars were really upmarket versions of Hillman cars from 1955 onwards, and its Sunbeam cars represented its sporting range, with the same bodyshells being used and only minor styling differences, often in the radiator grille. To satisfy BMC dealers who generally held either Austin or Morris/Nuffield franchises, the Austin and Morris cars shared the same engines and had the same level of equipment, whilst Wolseley cars had more standard equipment and MG cars more powerful engines. Riley cars generally combined the equipment levels of Wolseley cars with engines of the MG models.

It was not until the introduction of the Austin Maxi in 1968, and the Morris Marina in 1971, that the manufacturers' names started to represent different models once again. BMC (or British Motor Holdings (BMH) as it was now named) merged with the Leyland Motor Company, owner of Triumph and Rover, in 1968, and rationalisation of model names and ranges started to take place. The first casualty was Riley, which ceased to exist after 1969, with Wolseley and its final model, the 18/22, following in 1975. In 1969, Wolseley and Riley versions of the Mini were discontinued, and Austin and Morris badges disappeared as the Mini became a separate range in its own right. In 1984, the sole remaining Morris model, the Ital, was discontinued, leaving only Austin cars, which from 1987 were referred to as Austin/Rover models, with some even wearing Rover badges. In 1994, the last of the Austin cars, the Maestro and Montego, were discontinued. As well as cars, Austin did produce a few vans, mostly derived from the car range, and it should be remembered, whenever you see a London taxi, that Austin was supplying cars to be converted into taxis from the 1930s onwards, with taxis still bearing a resemblance to the Carbodies FX4 model of 1958 continuing to be made until the 1990s. Even as this book goes to press, scale models are still available for souvenir hunters wanting a little bit of London, and surely no toy museum would be complete without an Austin J40 pedal car.

Above: Bottom left of photograph are two Austin J40 pedal cars.
Right: Austin Taxi.
Below: A familiar car – the Austin Healey Frogeye Sprite. None of these, or any commercial vehicles, sports cars, the Princess Sheerline of the 1940s and '50s, or the Austin Champ and Gipsy, are covered in this book.

Austin A40 Dorset/Devon

Introduced in October 1947, the Dorset two-door saloon and Devon four-door saloon followed the standard 1940s practice of body-on-frame construction. Also common at this time were hydraulically-operated front brakes, with the rear brakes being operated mechanically. The engine was an OHV unit to replace the earlier side-valve, and the independent front suspension was also new. An interesting feature of these models was the use of a special jack, operated by the wheel brace from within the car, to lift one side. This method of jacking was continued on the Somerset, and involved leaving the door open whilst doing so – not ideal on modern roads, especially dual carriageways without any hard shoulder. Most of the early cars were destined for overseas markets, as they were made during a time when the Government was directing supplies of raw materials, such as steel, to companies which could demonstrate export capabilities. This was to help bring money into the country, to replace that which had been spent during the Second World War. The Dorset was dropped from the range in 1949.
Number produced: Dorset 15,939, Devon 2T3,590, Countryman estate 20,507.
Price when introduced: Dorset £403, Devon £416.
Standard equipment included ammeter, oil pressure gauge, glove box, parcel shelf, individual front seats, leather seats, central

Instrument layout.

Note the position of the handbrake under the steering column. Also, see the brake and clutch pedals protruding through the floor, not the pendant types associated with modern cars.

armrest in rear seat, and internal bonnet release.

Optional extras included heater, radio, sliding sunroof and more. Interestingly, a heater cost £5.25 but a sunroof was only an extra £3 (all prices exclude Purchase Tax).

COLOURS (1948): Portland grey, Royal blue, Mist green, Brown, Black.

COLOURS (1949): Portland grey, Seal grey, Solent blue, Mist green, Black.

ENGINE: Four-cylinder, OHV, bore 65.48mm, stroke 89mm, 1200cc (73.17in^3), maximum bhp 40 at 4300rpm, Zenith 30VM4 or 30VM5 carburettor.

GEARBOX: Four-speed, floor-mounted gear change, ratios: top 5.43, 3rd 8.33, 2nd 13.2, 1st 21.87, reverse 28.03.

REAR AXLE: Spiral bevel, three-quarter floating, ratio 5.43:1.

BRAKES: Girling, front hydraulic, rear mechanical, handbrake under facia near steering column.

STEERING: Cam and lever.

TYRES: Saloon 5.00 x 16, estate 5.00 x 17.

SUSPENSION: Front coil springs and wishbones, rear semi-elliptic leaf springs, anti-roll bar, front and rear double acting hydraulic shock absorbers.

DIMENSIONS: Devon saloon: length 12ft 9.25in (3.88m), width 5ft 1in (1.55m), height 5ft 3.75in (1.62m), wheelbase 7ft 8.5in (2.35m), track front 4ft 0.05in (1.23m), rear 4ft 1.5in (1.26m), ground clearance 6.75in (17cm), turning circle 38ft (11.4m), weight 19cwt 2lb (966kg).

CAPACITIES: Fuel 8.75 gallons (40 litres). Boot 7.4ft^3 (0.21m^3).

A40 Sports

The A40 Sports, based on the Devon, had an aluminium body, and was built from 1950 to 1953. Unlike earlier Austins, a convertible or, as it was more commonly known, 'Open Tourer' version of the Dorset/Devon was not available, so Austin turned to Jensen Motors which used a six-cylinder Austin engine in one of its own cars. Jensen, having previously redeveloped the bodywork of an Austin 7 during the 1920s, was asked by Austin to produce an Open Tourer using some of the mechanical components and chassis of the A40 saloons.

ENGINE: Four-cylinder, OHV, bore 65.48mm, stroke 89mm, 1200cc (73.17in^3), maximum bhp 46 at 5000rpm, two SU carburettors.
GEARBOX: Four-speed, column-mounted gear change, synchromesh on top three gears, ratios: top 5.14, 3rd 7.89, 2nd 12.52, 1st 20.00, reverse 27.68.
REAR AXLE: Spiral bevel, three-quarter floating.
BRAKES: Girling, hydraulic front and rear.
STEERING: Bishop cam and lever.
SUSPENSION: Front wishbones mounted on rubber bushes, independent coil springs, rear semi-elliptic leaf springs, anti-roll bar, front and rear Girling double acting shock absorbers.
TYRES: 5.25 x 16.
DIMENSIONS: Length 13ft 3.25in (4.04m), width 5ft 1in (1.55m), height 4ft 11in (1.5m), wheelbase 7ft 8.5in (2.35m), track front 4ft 0.5in (1.23m), rear 4ft 1.5in (1.26m), ground clearance 7.5in (19cm), turning circle 37ft (11.27m), approximate weight 19cwt (934kg).
CAPACITIES: Fuel 8.75 gallons (40 litres). Boot 13ft^3 (0.37m^3).

| AMP | FUEL | SPEEDO | OIL | TEMP |

Instrument layout.

Austin A40 Somerset

Introduced in February 1952 to replace the A40 Devon, the Somerset had a more rounded shape and, although retaining the same wheelbase, was longer and lower than its predecessor. A two-door convertible followed in late 1952 and ultimately replaced the A40 Sports, which was discontinued in 1953. There was no estate model to replace the Devon Countryman. The Somerset used the same body-on-frame construction as the Devon, and inherited its 1200cc engine, albeit with a slight increase in power, achieved by using the cylinder head from the A40 Sports, and a fully hydraulic brake system was now fitted. The Somerset was heavier than the Devon, so the increase in power was to help offset the greater weight. Together with the A70 Hereford, with which it shared its doors, the Somerset was the last of the body-on-frame cars from Austin; all future models were of monocoque construction. Although it had a more modern style, the Somerset never sold as well as the Devon. Alongside Australia and New Zealand, the Somerset was also assembled in Japan by Nissan. This was the second Austin car built by Nissan, the first being the Seven in 1934.

Number produced: 166,063 saloons, 7243 convertibles.

Instrument layout.

Indicator (trafficator) switch.

Price when introduced: Saloon £728, convertible £775.

Standard equipment included ammeter, oil pressure gauge, trip recorder, individual close-mounted front seats enabling use as a bench seat, leather seats, rear door armrests, and bonnet release and lock incorporated in flying 'A' bonnet motif. Optional extras included heater and radio.

ENGINE: Four-cylinder, OHV, bore 65.48mm, stroke 89mm, 1200cc (73.17in³), saloon maximum bhp 42 at 4500rpm, Zenith 30VIG8 carburettor.

GEARBOX: Ratios: top 5.28, 3rd 8.13, 2nd 12.88, 1st 20.54, reverse 28.56.

BRAKES: Girling, hydraulic front and rear.

STEERING: Bishop cam and lever.

TYRES: 5.25 x 16

SUSPENSION: Front, unequal length wishbones, coil springs and Armstrong shock absorbers, rear semi-elliptic leaf springs, anti-roll bar, lever-arm shock absorbers.

DIMENSIONS: Length 13ft 3.5in (4.05m), width 5ft 3in (1.6m), height 5ft 4in (1.63m), convertible 5ft 2.5in (1.588m), wheelbase 7ft 8.5in (2.35m), track front 4ft 0.0625in (1.22m), rear 4ft 2in (1.27m), ground clearance 7.5in (19cm), turning circle 37ft (11.28m), weight 19cwt 14lb (971kg).

CAPACITIES. Fuel 8.75 gallons (40 litres). Boot 10ft³ (0.28m³).

Gear change diagram.

Austin A70 Hampshire

Introduced in September 1948, a year after the Devon and at first glance appearing to have similar styling, the Hampshire was wider and longer, with the front lights further inset. It had a larger boot and rear wheel spats. It also had a larger engine, however, unlike the Devon, this was not a new engine; it had already been used in an earlier car – the Austin 16. The Hampshire was available as a saloon, estate and pickup. The Countryman estate had semi-wooden bodywork and was built as a specific model, unlike the Devon whose Countryman estate was effectively a van with windows.
Number produced: 34,360 saloons, 901 estates.
Price in 1949: Standard saloon £507 plus £141.58 Purchase Tax, with sliding sunroof £515 plus £143.80 Purchase Tax, estate £595 plus £166 Purchase Tax.
Standard equipment included, ammeter, oil pressure gauge, heater, two glove boxes, split front bench seat with individual adjustment for each half, leather or leather and cloth upholstery, front door pockets, central armrest in rear seat, internal bonnet release, and a comprehensive tool kit fitted into the boot lid. Interestingly, unlike the Devon, it did not have a water temperature gauge. Optional extras included radio, sliding sunroof and more.

ENGINE: Four-cylinder, OHV, bore 79.4mm, stroke 111.1mm, 2199cc (134.19in³), maximum bhp 68 at 3800rpm, Zenith 42VIS carburettor.
GEARBOX: Four-speed, steering column gear change, synchromesh on top three gears,

ratios: top 4.125, 3rd 5.84, 2nd 9.28, 1st 15.34, reverse 19.73.
REAR AXLE: Spiral bevel, three-quarter floating, ratio 4.125:1.
BRAKES: Girling, front hydraulic, rear mechanical, pistol grip type handbrake mounted on underside of steering column.
STEERING: Cam and lever.
SUSPENSION: Front, coil springs and wishbones, rear semi-elliptic leaf springs, anti-roll bar, front and rear double acting hydraulic shock absorbers.
TYRES: Saloon 5.50 x 16, Countryman 5.75 x 16.
DIMENSIONS: Saloon, length 13ft 7.25in (4.15m), width 5ft 6.375in (1.69m), height 5ft 5in (1.65m), wheelbase 8ft (2.43m), track front 4ft 5.5in (1.35m), rear 4ft 7.5in (1.4m) ground clearance 6.5in (16.5cm), turning circle 39ft (11.88m), weight 1 ton 5cwt (1270kg).
CAPACITIES: Fuel 12.5 gallons (56.8 litres). Boot 9.5ft³ (0.27m³).

Austin A70 Hereford

Introduced in October 1950 to replace the Hampshire, there were some technical changes with both front and rear brakes now hydraulically operated, and the list of standard equipment was extended to include a water temperature gauge and clock, and footrests for rear seat passengers were incorporated at the rear of the front seats. Although it had similar styling to the Somerset, the Hereford can be easily identified by an oval vent on the sides of the bonnet, near the front doors, with 'Austin of England' on it. Models available were a saloon, estate and pickup. Like the Hampshire, the Countryman estate had combined steel and wood bodywork. A further model, a convertible, was built by Carbodies of Coventry.

Number produced: 48,640 saloons, 266 convertibles, 1515 estates.

Price when introduced: including Purchase Tax, saloon £738, convertible £1122. Standard equipment included, ammeter, oil pressure gauge, clock, heater, two glove boxes, split front bench seat with individual adjustment for each half, leather trimmed seats, front and rear door pockets and armrests, central armrest in rear seat, and internal bonnet release. Optional extras included radio, and sliding steel sunroof.

ENGINE: Four-cylinder, OHV, bore 79.4mm, stroke 111.1mm, 2199cc (134.19in^3), maximum bhp 68 at 3800rpm, Zenith 42VIS carburettor.

GEARBOX: Four-speed, column gear change, synchromesh on top three gears, ratios: top 4.125, 3rd 5.85, 2nd 9.28, 1st 14.83, reverse 20.53.

REAR AXLE: Spiral bevel, three-quarter floating, ratio 4.125:1.

This car has had indicators fitted beneath the rear bumper.

BRAKES: Girling, hydraulic front and rear, pistol grip type handbrake mounted on underside of steering column.

STEERING: Cam and lever.

SUSPENSION: Front, coil springs and wishbones, rear semi-elliptic leaf springs, anti-roll bar, front and rear double acting hydraulic shock absorbers.

TYRES: 5.50 x 16.

DIMENSIONS: Length 13ft 11.5in (4.25m), width 5ft 9.375in (1.77m), height 5ft 5.75in (1.67m), wheelbase 8ft 3in (2.51m), track front 4ft 5.565in (1.36m), rear 4ft 8in (1.42m), ground clearance 7.5in (19cm), turning circle 39ft (11.89m), weight 1 ton 4cwt 1qtr 10lb (1241kg).

CAPACITIES: Fuel 12.5 gallons (56.8 litres). Boot 10ft^3 (0.28m^3).

Austin A90 Atlantic

Introduced as a convertible in September 1948, and as a saloon in September 1949. The convertible was discontinued in November 1950, the saloon in December 1952. Aimed at the American market, the Atlantic was designed by Dick Burzi using the chassis and many mechanical

components from the A70 Hampshire, but it had a larger engine.
Number produced: 7981.
Standard equipment included water temperature and oil pressure gauges, ammeter, revolution counter, two glove boxes, two sun visors with mirror on passenger visor, individual close-mounted front seats trimmed in leather, side and central armrests for rear seat, internal bonnet release, and more.

ENGINE: Four-cylinder, OHV, bore 87.3mm, stroke 111.1mm, 2660cc (162.2in³), maximum bhp 88, two SU H4 carburettors.
GEARBOX: Ratios as A70 Hampshire.
BRAKES: Girling, hydraulic/mechanical.

STEERING: Bishop cam and lever.
TYRES: 5.50 x 16.
SUSPENSION: As A70 Hampshire.
DIMENSIONS: Length 14ft 9in (4.5m), width 5ft 10in (1.78m), height coupé 5ft 1in (1.55m), convertible 5ft 0in (1.524m), wheelbase 8ft 0in (2.44m), track front 4ft 5.5in (1.35m), rear 4ft 7.5in (1.4m), ground clearance 7.5in (19cm), turning circle 39ft (11.88m), weight 1 ton 6cwt 3qtr (1359kg).
CAPACITIES: Fuel 12.5 gallons (56 litres).

Austin Metropolitan

Introduced in 1954, the Metropolitan was the result of an agreement between Austin and the American car company Nash Kelvinator, whereby Nash, with the help of independent stylist William Flajole, designed the body and Austin built the cars. Donald Healey, who had previously worked with Nash (to produce the Nash Healey roadster) and Austin (to produce the Austin Healey sports car) introduced the two companies. The original engine, a 1200cc unit, was ultimately replaced by the B-series 1489cc engine in 1956, the same year that the Metropolitan underwent a substantial restyle to the front

Above, some cars have the spare wheel exposed to the elements whilst others have fabric covers.

end and sides of the car, receiving a novel side trim ideally suited for two-tone paint schemes. Later changes included the fitment of quarter lights in the doors, and an external opening boot lid. It was available as a hard top coupé and convertible, and was bought not only by private individuals but also by American companies for use as fleet cars, and by police forces to replace the motor cycles often used by parking enforcement officers. The bodies were built by Fisher & Ludlow, then transported to Austin for mechanical components to be fitted, and then final assembly. It was originally sold as a Nash or Hudson model, but following the creation of the American Motors Corporation (AMC) it became known simply as the Metropolitan, and was distributed by Rambler dealers. Sales in the UK commenced in 1957, and it was discontinued in 1961. Total sales in the USA and Canada were approximately 95,000, plus 9400 for the UK and Europe. Optional extras on the early cars included heater, radio, and whitewall tyres. UK cars had a heater and radio as standard, the instrumentation, however, remained just a speedometer and fuel gauge.

COLOURS (1954): Two-tone all with upper roof in Mist grey. Then a choice of Spruce green, Croton green, Canyon red, Caribbean blue.
COLOURS (1956): Two-tone all with Snowberry white roof and lower half. For centre section, choice of Caribbean green, Sunburst yellow, Coral red, Black.
ENGINE (1954): Four-cylinder, OHV, bore 65.48mm, stroke 88.9mm, 1200cc (73.17in^3), maximum bhp 42 at 4500rpm, Zenith carburettor.

GEARBOX: Three-speed, steering column mounted gear change, ratios: top 4.625, 2nd 7.099, 1st 11.267, reverse 16.137.
REAR AXLE: Spiral bevel, ratio 4.625:1.
BRAKES: Girling, hydraulic, front and rear 8-inch drums.
STEERING: Cam and lever.
TYRES: 5.20 x 13.
SUSPENSION: Front independent coil springs, rear semi-elliptic leaf springs.
DIMENSIONS: Length 12ft 5.4in (3.794m), width 5ft 1.5in (1.562m), height 4ft 6.4in (1.381m), wheelbase 7ft 1in (2.159m), track front 3ft 9.3in, (1.15m), rear 3ft 8.8in (1.138m), ground clearance 6in (15.24cm), turning circle 34ft approx (10.46m), weight 16cwt 2qtr 21lb (849kg).
CAPACITIES: Fuel 9.5 gallons (43 litres).

Metropolitan 1500
As earlier models except:
ENGINE: Four-cylinder, OHV, bore 73mm, stroke 88.9mm, 1489cc (90.9in^3), maximum bhp 52 at 4500rpm, Zenith 30VIG10 carburettor.
GEARBOX: Ratios with 4.3 final drive: top 4.3, 2nd 6.4, 1st 12.2.
REAR AXLE: Hypoid bevel, ratio 4.3:1, later 1500 cars 4.22:1.
TYRES: Later cars 5.60 x 13.
DIMENSIONS: Length 12ft 5.5in (3.797m), height coupé 4ft 8in (1.422m), convertible 4ft 8.5in (1.435m), ground clearance 6.75in (17.14cm), weight coupé 16cwt 3qtr 9lb (856kg), convertible 16cwt 3qtr (852kg).
CAPACITIES: Fuel 8.75 gallons (40 litres).

Austin A30

Introduced at the 1951 Motor Show, the Austin A30 Seven, which was the first Austin to feature a monocoque body, bore a passing resemblance to a small Austin Hereford, which had been designed by Dick Burzi. The A30 was initially available as a four-door saloon (a two-door model followed in late 1953, and an estate and van in 1954), and featured a new OHV engine of 803cc. This engine would become known as the 'A-series,' and in 848cc guise would power another Seven – the Mini – in 1959. By this time it had already found its way into the Austin Healey Sprite sports car. At a time when many manufacturers were using three-speed gearboxes, the four-speed unit fitted to the A30, together with its floor-mounted gear change, was innovative. Not so new, however, were the semaphore indicators, which swung out from the pillar behind the front doors, but many cars have now been fitted with modern flashing indicators by later owners. Acceleration times of around 40 seconds to reach 60mph were, by modern standards, slow, but despite this the A30 was a popular car on the race track, the rear axle ratios being changed at various times during its life. Other changes included revisions to seats and door panels, and moving the optional heater under the bonnet to increase interior space. Modifications to the boot included moving the positions of the spare wheel, fuel filler and hinges to increase boot capacity. These changes can be seen by comparing the rear of the earlier black and later grey cars.

Number produced: 223,264
Price when introduced: Four-door saloon £507.

Standard equipment included front bucket seats, leather cloth trim, opening front and rear quarter lights, pull-up door windows. Later cars had a front parcel shelf instead of two glove boxes. Optional extras included a heater.

Instrument layout.

COLOURS (1952): Cotswold beige, Dove grey, Austin Seven grey, Selsy blue, Sedgemoor green, Sandown fawn, Shaftesbury grey, Black.

COLOURS (1953): Introduced in 1953 were two-tone colour schemes for two-door models: Coronet cream with red or Sandringham fawn roof; Balmoral blue with Windsor grey or Chelsea grey roof; Chelsea grey with blue, Coronet cream or Sandringham fawn roof; Windsor grey with Balmoral blue roof. Black however remained a popular choice, especially for four-door cars.

COLOURS (1956): Tintern green, Spruce green, Cardigan grey, Chelsea grey, Tweed grey, Conway blue, Streamline blue.

ENGINE: Four-cylinder, OHV, bore 58mm, stroke 76mm, 803cc (48.8in^3), maximum bhp 28 at 4800rpm, Zenith 26 JS carburettor.

GEARBOX: Four-speed, floor-mounted gear change, synchromesh on top three gears, ratios: top 1.00, 3rd 1.68, 2nd 2.59, 1st 4.09, giving overall ratios of top 5.14, 3rd 8.64, 2nd 13.32, 1st 21.03, reverse 26.63 for early models with 5.14 final drive.

REAR AXLE: Hypoid bevel, three-quarter floating, ratio on early cars 5.14:1, subsequently changed to 5.125, 4.875 and finally 5.375.

BRAKES: Lockheed hydraulic, front and rear 7-inch drums.

STEERING: Cam and lever.

TYRES: 5.20 x 13.

SUSPENSION: Front, independent coil springs and wishbones, rear semi-elliptic leaf springs, anti-roll bar, front and rear double acting hydraulic shock absorbers.

DIMENSIONS: Length 11ft 4.375 (3.46m), width 4ft 7.125in (1.4m), height 4ft 10.25in (1.48m), wheelbase 6ft 7.5in (2.02m), track front 3ft 9.25in (1.15m), rear 3ft 8.75in (1.14m), ground clearance 6.375in (17cm), turning circle 35ft (10.67m), weight 13cwt 2qtr (698kg) approximately.

CAPACITIES: Fuel 5.75 gallons (26.14 litres).

Gear change diagram.

Austin A35

Introduced in 1956 to replace the A30, it is easily identifiable by its front grille (now painted in the body colour with a chrome surround), a larger rear window, and amber front and rear indicators instead of the semaphore type. It also featured a larger engine and shorter gear change lever, but brakes were still a combination of fully hydraulic front and mixed hydraulic and mechanical rear, and pedals were still of the non-pendant type. Also retained was the 'Flying A' bonnet badge (which incorporated the bonnet release catch), a combined door handle and window lock with pull-up windows in the front doors, and, on four-door cars, the pillar between the doors still had the space for the original A30 indicators, albeit covered by a blanking plate. The A35 was available as a Standard or De Luxe saloon with two or four doors, a Countryman estate, van, and pickup. The van continued to be built until 1968 with a variety of engines. The cars were discontinued in 1959.
Number produced: Two-door saloons 100,284, four-door saloons 28,961, pickup 475, Countryman estates 5780, vans 210,000 approximately. A number of CKD cars were also sent overseas for assembly.
Price when introduced: Two-door saloon £541, four-door saloon £574, Countryman £639.
Standard equipment included front bucket seats trimmed in PVC, rubber mat in front and carpet in rear, opening front and rear quarter lights, full-width front parcel shelf. De Luxe models also had ashtrays, overriders, and hinged opening rear windows on two-door models. Optional extras included a heater and radio.

Instrument layout.

COLOURS (1956): Island blue, Streamline blue, Capri blue, Spruce green, Tintern green, Court grey, Tweed grey, Chelsea grey, Black.

COLOURS (1959): Island blue, Speedwell blue, Spruce green, Palm green, Court grey, Tweed grey, Black.

ENGINE: Four-cylinder, OHV, bore 62.9mm, stroke 76.2mm, 948cc (57.82in^3), maximum bhp 34 at 4750rpm, Zenith 26VME carburettor.

GEARBOX: Four-speed, floor-mounted gear change, synchromesh on top three gears, ratios: top 4.55, 3rd 6.42, 2nd 10.79, 1st 16.50, reverse 21.22.

REAR AXLE: Hypoid bevel, three-quarter floating, ratio 4.55:1.

BRAKES: Lockheed hydraulic, front and rear 7-inch drum.

STEERING: Cam and peg.

TYRES: Saloon 5.20 x 13, estate and commercials 5.60 x 13, optional 5.90 x 13.

SUSPENSION: Front independent coil springs and wishbones, rear semi-elliptic leaf springs, anti-roll bar, front and rear hydraulic lever-arm shock absorbers.

Gear change diagram.

A late model van: 1967 registration.

DIMENSIONS: Length 11ft 4.375 (3.46m), width 4ft 7.125in (1.4m), height 4ft 11.25in (1.50m), wheelbase 6ft 7.5in (2.02m), track front 3ft 9.25in (1.15m), rear 3ft 8.75in (1.14m), ground clearance 6.375in (17cm), turning circle 35ft (10.67m), weight two-door 13cwt 2qtr (686kg), four-door 13cwt 2qtr 14lb (692kg), all weights unladen without fuel.
CAPACITIES: Fuel 5.75 gallons (26.14 litres).
ENGINES (Later van): All four-cylinder, OHV. From 1962 to 1966: bore 64.6mm, stroke 83.7mm, 1098cc (67.0in³), maximum bhp 48 at 5100rpm (high compression 8.5:1) or bhp 45 at 5100rpm (low compression 7.5:1). From 1964 to 1968: bore 62.94mm, stroke 68.26mm, 848cc (51.7in³), maximum bhp 34 at 5500rpm. Both engines with SU HS2 carburettors.
REAR AXLE: Ratios 4.222:1 with 1098cc engine, 4.875:1 with 848cc engine.

Austin A40/A50 Cambridge

Introduced in 1954 with identical bodies but different engines, the A40 and A50 Cambridge replaced the A40 Somerset. Available as a saloon car, van, and pickup, this was the second of the Austin cars to use the monocoque, or as it is also known, unitary construction body, the first car being the A30. Although a two-door version of the A40/A50 was considered, only a few were manufactured as a design exercise. However, some brochures include a reference to Family and De Luxe two-door cars, and the four-door cars were called Standard and De Luxe. Improvements over the Somerset included larger brakes and boot. It was three-inches longer and had a seven-inch longer wheelbase, and although the overall width was reduced, the new design, with its upright sides, had greater interior width with wider seats. However, it lost the ammeter and oil pressure gauges. The Cambridge was produced in Japan by Nissan, and pickups were built in Australia. The A40 was discontinued in 1956, the A50 in 1957.
Number produced: A40 30,666, A50 114,867, including vans and pickups.
Price when introduced: A40 Standard £664, De Luxe £707, A50 Standard £678, De Luxe £721.

Standard equipment included fuel and water temperature gauges, trip mileage recorder, seats with PVC coated fabric, driver's sun visor, rubber floor covering in front and carpet in rear, full-width front parcel shelf, glove box on passenger side, and opening front and rear quarter lights. De Luxe added a heater, leather trimmed seats, carpet in front instead of rubber, arm rests on doors, passenger sun visor, locking glove box lid, twin horns, overriders, and chromium

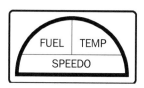

Instrument layout.

mouldings. Optional extras included radio, clock, manumatic (automatic) transmission, overdrive and more.

ENGINE (A40): Four-cylinder, OHV, bore 65.48mm, stroke 89mm, 1200cc ($73.17in^3$), maximum bhp 42 at 4500rpm, Zenith 30VIG carburettor.

ENGINE (A50): Four-cylinder, OHV, bore 73.025mm, stroke 89mm, 1489cc ($90.88in^3$), maximum bhp 50 at 4400rpm, Zenith 30VIG10 carburettor.

GEARBOX: Four-speed, steering column mounted gear change, synchromesh on top three gears, A40 ratios: top 5.125, 3rd 7.64, 2nd 12.31, 1st 20.22, reverse 26.44. A50 ratios: o/d top 3.42, top 4.875, o/d 3rd 5.08, 3rd 7.06, 2nd 11.71, 1st 19.23, reverse 25.15. Later A50: top 4.30, 3rd 6.41, 2nd 10.30, 1st 16.96, reverse 22.18.

REAR AXLE: Hypoid bevel, ratios A40: 5.125:1. A50 early cars and all overdrive models: 4.875:1, later cars 4.3:1.

BRAKES: Girling, hydraulic, front and rear 9-inch drums, handbrake incorporated in steering column.

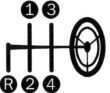

All images on this page are of an A40.

Gear change diagram.

STEERING: Cam and peg.
TYRES: 5.60 x 15, later cars 5.90 x 13.
SUSPENSION: Front independent coil springs and wishbones, rear semi-elliptic leaf springs, anti-roll bar, front and rear double acting hydraulic shock absorbers.
DIMENSIONS: Length 13ft 6.25in (4.11m), width 5ft 1.5in (1.55m), height 5ft 0.5in (1.54m), wheelbase 8ft 3.25in (2.51m), track front 4ft 0.5in (1.22m), rear 4ft 1in (1.24m), ground clearance 6in (15cm), turning circle 36ft (11m).
CAPACITIES: Fuel 8.75 gallons (39.7 litres). Boot 14ft^3 (0.4m^3).

All images on this page are of A50s.

23

Austin A55 Cambridge

Introduced in 1957 to replace the A50. The A40 had been deleted from the Austin range in 1956 and was not replaced. The A55 used the same engine as the A50, but had a higher compression ratio and developed more power. New was a longer, restyled body, with larger boot, rear window and tail fins, incorporating vertically-mounted rear lights. A chrome side strip enabled the use of an optional two-tone paint scheme, with the lower half, roof and boot of the car painted in one colour, and the centre section, including the bonnet, painted in another. Two saloon models were available from the start: Standard and De Luxe, with the van, pickup and chassis/cab versions arriving in 1958. These proved popular with coachbuilding companies, who converted them into motor homes. The commercial versions of the A55 continued to be made until 1971, with some wearing Morris badges.

Number produced: 154,000 to 1958, including van and pickup models.

Price when introduced: De Luxe £820. Standard equipment included water temperature gauge, trip mileage recorder, PVC trimmed seats, driver's sun visor, rubber mat in front, carpet in rear, full-width front parcel shelf, glove box on passenger side, and opening front and rear quarter

lights. De Luxe added a heater, leather trimmed seats, carpet in front instead of rubber, armrests on doors, passenger sun visor, twin horns, and overriders. Optional extras included, radio, clock, Manumatic (automatic) transmission, overdrive, two-tone paint finish and more.

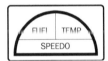

Instrument layout.

COLOURS (1958): Court grey, Tweed grey, Speedwell blue, Kingfisher blue, Palm green, Black. Two-tone options (roof, boot, lower body colour first): Court grey/Island blue, Tweed grey/Court grey, Palm green/Spruce green, Speedwell blue/Island blue.

ENGINE: Four-cylinder, OHV, bore 73.025mm, stroke 89mm, 1489cc (90.88in^3), maximum 51bhp at 4250rpm, Zenith 30VIG10 carburettor.

GEARBOX: Four-speed, steering column mounted gear change, synchromesh on top three gears, ratios: top 4.30, 3rd 6.41, 2nd 10.33, 1st 16.96, reverse 22.18. With optional overdrive, ratios: o/d top 3.413, top 4.875, o/d 3rd 5.08, 3rd 7.06, 2nd 11.71, 1st 19.23, reverse 25.15.

REAR AXLE: Hypoid bevel, ratios 4.3:1, with optional overdrive 4.875:1.

BRAKES: Girling, hydraulic, front and rear 9-inch drums, handbrake adjacent to steering column.

STEERING: Cam and peg.

TYRES: 5.90 x 13.

SUSPENSION: Front independent coil springs and wishbones, rear semi-elliptic leaf springs, anti-roll bar, front and rear hydraulic lever type shock absorbers.

DIMENSIONS: Length 13ft 10.875in (4.24m), width 5ft 1.5in (1.55m), height 5ft 0.25in

Note the revised front grille for later models.

(1.53m), wheelbase 8ft 3.25in (2.51m), track front 4ft 0.5in (1.22m) rear 4ft 1in (1.24m), ground clearance 6.375in (16cm), turning circle 36ft (11m), weight 1 ton 2qtr 14lb (1048kg).

CAPACITIES: Fuel 8.75 gallons (39.7 litres). Boot 14.5ft^3 (0.41m^3).

Austin A90 Six Westminster/ A105 Six

The A90 was introduced in 1954 to replace the A70 Hampshire. The Westminster appeared at the same time as the A40/A50 cars; it had the same styling and used their doors, but it was longer and wider, and had a six-cylinder engine, the new BMC 'C-series.' A more powerful version of this engine was used in an additional Westminster model, the A105 Six, which was launched in 1956. Also at this time, the engine was fitted to the Austin Healey 100/6 sports car. The A90 was available as a Standard or De Luxe model, but only one version of the A105 was offered. It had more equipment than the A90 De Luxe and was available with a two-tone paint scheme, with the roof and lower body painted one colour, the centre section, including the bonnet and boot lid, in another.

Number produced: A90 25,532, A105 1000 approximately.

Price when introduced: A90 Standard £792, A90 De Luxe £834, A105 £1109. Standard equipment for the A90 included water temperature and oil pressure gauges, trip mileage recorder, PVC trimmed seats (which can be aligned to form a bench seat to accommodate three people), sun visors, rubber mat in front, carpet in rear, full-width parcel shelf, glove box on passenger side, opening front and rear quarter lights, and internal bonnet release. The A90 De Luxe added a heater, clock, leather trimmed seats, carpet in front instead of rubber, armrests, locking glove box lid, and overriders. The A105, in addition to the features of the A90 De Luxe, had two foglights, two wing mirrors, windscreen washers, and overdrive. Optional extras included radio and, where not fitted as standard, heater, clock, wing mirrors and more.

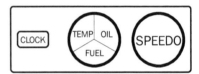

Instrument layout, including clock as fitted to A90 De Luxe and A105.

The car pictured top is an A90 with extra bonnet vents; the car above is an A105.

ENGINE (A90): Six-cylinder, OHV, bore 79.4mm, stroke 89mm, 2639cc (160.91in^3), maximum bhp 85 at 4300rpm, Zenith 42VIS carburettor.

ENGINE (A105): Six-cylinder, OHV, bore 79.4mm, stroke 89mm, 2639cc (160.91in^3), maximum bhp 102 at 4600rpm, two SU H4 carburettors.

GEARBOX: Four-speed, steering column mounted gear change, synchromesh on top three gears. A90 ratios: top 3.91, 3rd 5.61, 2nd 8.055, 1st 12.96, reverse 17.569. A105 ratios: o/d top 2.87, top 4.10, o/d 3rd 4.12, 3rd 5.89, 2nd 9.10, 1st 13.57, reverse 18.42.

REAR AXLE: Hypoid bevel, ratios A90, 3.9:1, A105, 4.1:1.

BRAKES: Girling, hydraulic, front and rear 11-inch drums, handbrake incorporated in steering column.

STEERING: Cam and peg.

TYRES: 6.40 x 15.

SUSPENSION: Front independent coil springs and wishbones, rear semi-elliptic leaf springs, anti-roll bar, front and rear double acting hydraulic shock absorbers.

DIMENSIONS: Length 14ft 2.25in (4.33m), width 5ft 1.5in (1.55m), height 5ft 4in

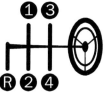

Gear change diagram.

(1.63m), wheelbase 8ft 7.75in (2.64m), track front 4ft 3.5in (1.31m), rear 4ft 3.25in (1.30m), ground clearance 7.75in (19cm), turning circle 36ft (11m), weight A90 1 ton 5cwt 2qtr (1295kg), A105 1 ton 6cwt (1320kg).

CAPACITIES: Fuel 12.5 gallons (56.82 litres). Boot 14.0ft^3 (0.40m^3).

Austin A95 Six Westminster/A105

Introduced in 1957 to replace the A90 and previous A105, the Westminster name disappeared from some brochures. Just as the previous cars had been styled like the A50, the new A95/A105 followed the styling of the A55. As had been the case with the A90 and previous A105, there were three saloon models, but there was a new additional model – the A95 estate. It had the same equipment levels as the A95 De Luxe saloon, and, in true Austin style, the estate was called the Countryman, a name that was also used on the last Austin estate model, the Montego. For a while, there was also a Vanden Plas version of the A105, which featured different trim, and had discreet exterior badges. The two-tone paint scheme for the early A95 saloon and estate consisted of a different coloured side flash, whereas the A105 models always had the roof painted the same colour as the side

All cars in this section are A105 Six.

flash. The paint scheme was completely different to the A55, which had a similar but not identical style to the previous A105. The A95 and A105 were both discontinued in 1959, and replaced by the Farina-styled A99.

Left: Vanden Plas front wing trim
Right: standard A105 Six front wing trim.

Number produced: A95 28,065, A105 5270 approximately.
Price when introduced: A95 saloon £999, A95 estate £1216, A105 £1200.
Standard equipment on the A95 included water temperature and oil pressure gauges, trip mileage recorder, PVC trimmed seats (which can be aligned to form a bench seat

to accommodate three people), sun visors, rubber mat in front, carpet in rear, full-width parcel shelf, glove box on passenger side, opening front and rear quarter lights, and internal bonnet release. The A95 De Luxe added a heater, clock, leather trimmed

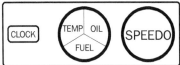

Instrument layout, including clock as fitted to A95 De Luxe and A105.

A Vanden Plas 105 Six model.

Lockable fuel filler cap.

seats, carpet in front instead of rubber, chrome window mouldings, and overriders. The A105, in addition to the features of the A95 De Luxe, had two foglights, windscreen washers, Borg-Warner overdrive, and two-tone paint scheme. Note: the A95 estate did not have opening quarter lights in rear door. Optional extras included radio, and where not fitted as standard, heater, clock, wing mirrors and more.

ENGINE (A95): Six-cylinder, OHV, bore 79.4mm, stroke 89mm, 2639cc (160.91in³), maximum bhp 92 at 4500rpm, Zenith 42VIS carburettor.
ENGINE (A105): Six-cylinder, OHV, bore 79.4mm, stroke 89mm, 2639cc (160.91in³), maximum bhp 102 at 4600rpm, two SU H4 carburettors.
GEARBOX: Four-speed, steering column mounted gear change, synchromesh on top three gears, A95 ratios: top 3.91, 3rd 5.597, 2nd 8.658, 1st 12.917, reverse 17.523. A105 ratios: o/d top 2.87, top 4.10, o/d 3rd 4.12, 3rd 5.88, 2nd 9.10, 1st 13.58, reverse 18.42. A95 estate ratios as A105, except no overdrive fitted.
REAR AXLE: Hypoid bevel, ratios: A95 saloon 3.9:1, A95 estate and A105 4.1:1.
BRAKES: Girling, hydraulic, front and rear 11-inch drums, handbrake incorporated in steering column.

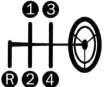

Gear change diagram.

STEERING: Cam and peg.
TYRES: 6.40 x 15, estate 6.70 x 15.
SUSPENSION: Front independent coil springs and wishbones, rear semi-elliptic leaf springs, anti-roll bar, front and rear hydraulic lever type shock absorbers.
DIMENSIONS: Length 15ft 0.75in (4.58m), width 5ft 4in (1.63m), height 5ft 2in (1.57m), wheelbase 8ft 9.75in (2.68m), track front 4ft 3.5in (1.31m), rear 4ft 3.25in (1.30m), ground clearance 7in (18cm), turning circle 40ft (12.19m), weight A95 1 ton 5cwt 3qtr (1308kg), A105 1 ton 6cwt (1321kg).
CAPACITIES: Fuel 16 gallons (72.7 litres). Boot 14.5ft³ (0.41m³), estate with rear seat folded down 62ft³ (1.76m³).

Austin A40 mark 1

The A40 was introduced in 1958, marginally ahead of the Wolseley 15/60, which many people often consider the first of the Farina-styled BMC cars to be launched. Another point of note is that whatever the original intentions, the A40 did not directly replace the A35, which continued in production until August 1959 when the Austin Seven – or Mini as it soon became known – was introduced to take over as the new small Austin. The A40 designation was originally used in 1947 for the Austin Devon model, which was replaced in 1952 by the Somerset, and ultimately by the A40 Cambridge in 1954. The Cambridge name continued to be used for many years, and was subsequently applied to another Farina-styled car, the A55 of 1959. The A40 was also produced in Italy by Innocenti of Milan, perhaps rather appropriate given that the styling had originally been done by an Italian company. The A40 used most of the mechanical components of the A35, including the legendary A-series engine, which ultimately went on to power the Mini and the Austin Healey Sprite sports car. Unlike the A35, the A40 was only available as a two-door saloon. It did, however, have a fold down rear seat, and became available as an estate car in late 1959.

Other differences from the A35 included pendant type brake and clutch pedals. As was common practice from the 1950s onwards, the A40 was available as a Basic or De Luxe model with additional equipment, but whichever model was ordered, a heater was an optional extra. Improvements during 1959 included self-cancelling indicators,

Instrument layout.

and a lid was placed over the spare wheel to create a flat floor in the boot.

Number produced: 141,897 saloons, 27,715 Countryman estates.

Price in 1959: De Luxe saloon £651, estate £672.

Standard equipment included adjustable front seats, fold down rear seat, rubber floor mat, and driver's sun visor. De Luxe versions came with passenger sun visor, opening rear side windows, overriders, and stainless steel windscreen and window surrounds. Optional extras on all models were radio, heater, and screen washers.

No window winders; glass had to be pulled up.

Gear change diagram.

COLOURS: All with black roof: Farina grey, Tartan red, Horizon blue, Ocean blue, Sutherland green.

ENGINE: Four-cylinder, OHV, bore 62.9mm, stroke 76.2mm, 948cc (57.82in^3), maximum bhp 34 at 4670rpm, Zenith 26VME, carburettor.

GEARBOX: Four-speed, floor-mounted gear change, synchromesh on top three gears, ratios: top 4.55, 3rd 6.42, 2nd 10.79, 1st 16.51, reverse 21.22.

REAR AXLE: Hypoid bevel, three-quarter floating, ratio 4.55:1.

BRAKES: Lockheed, front hydraulically operated 8-inch drums, rear mechanically operated 7-inch drums. Handbrake between front seats.

STEERING: Cam and peg.

TYRES: Saloon 5.20 x 13, estate 5.90 x 13.

SUSPENSION: Front independent with coil springs and wishbones, rear semi-elliptic leaf springs, lever type hydraulic shock absorbers.

DIMENSIONS: Length with overriders 12ft 2in (3.71m), width 4ft 11.375in (1.51m), height 4ft 8.75in (1.44m), wheelbase 6ft 11.5in (2.12m), kerb weight 14cwt 1qtr 14lb (730kg).

CAPACITIES: Fuel 6 gallons (27 litres).

Austin A40 mark 2

Introduced in October 1961 to replace the mark 1, changes included a redesigned radiator grille, repositioned rear boot badges, wind-up (as opposed to lift up) windows were fitted to the doors, and a heater was now standard on the De Luxe model. Other improvements included a lengthened wheelbase, achieved by moving the axle further back on the leaf springs. This also allowed the rear seat to be moved back, increasing rear seat legroom. Further additions were fully hydraulic braking (replacing the previous mixed hydraulic/mechanical system), a front anti-roll bar, and telescopic shock absorbers, which replaced the lever-arm type. Power was increased by fitting an SU carburettor, and was increased again a year later in 1962, when a 1098cc engine replaced the 948cc unit. Also at this time, changes were made to the transmission, with improved synchromesh for the gearbox and a revised rear axle ratio. The A40 mark 2 was discontinued in 1967 and not replaced. With the public turning to front-wheel drive, the similar sized Austin 1100/1300 was now the popular choice. **Number produced:** (948cc) 35,133 saloon, 14,744 estate. (1098cc) 74,119 saloon, 35,529 estate.

Instrument layout.

Price when introduced: (948cc) saloon £654, estate £675, (1098cc) saloon £599, estate £617. A reduction in Purchase Tax during 1962 lowered the price of all cars. Standard equipment included adjustable front seats, fold down rear seat, rubber floor

mat, driver's sun visor, wind-up windows, hinged rear seat cushions, and from 1964 a revised facia. De Luxe added a heater, water temperature gauge, windscreen washers, carpet, passenger sun visor, opening rear side windows, overriders, and stainless steel windscreen and window surrounds. Countryman estate added wing mirrors, and opening rear window. Optional extras on all models were radio, two-tone paint, stainless steel wheel trims, basic model heater, windscreen washers and more.

COLOURS (1962): Main body colour/roof: Horizon blue/Black, Agate red/Black, Fern green/Snowberry white, Cumulus grey/Snowberry white, Snowberry white/Cumulus grey. Single tone only: Maroon.
COLOURS (1963 on): In addition to 1962 colours: Embassy maroon/Black, Black/Cumulus grey. Single tone: Black. Note: Glen green replaced Fern green from 1964 onwards.

1962 specification
ENGINE: Four-cylinder, OHV, bore 64.58mm, stroke 83.72mm, 1098cc (66.98in^3), maximum bhp 48 at 5100rpm, SU HS2 carburettor.

GEARBOX: Four-speed, floor-mounted gear change, synchromesh on top three gears, ratios: top 4.22, 3rd 5.95, 2nd 9.16, 1st 15.32, reverse 21.22.
REAR AXLE: Hypoid bevel, three-quarter floating, ratio 4.22:1.
BRAKES: Fully hydraulic, front 8-inch drums, rear 7-inch drums. Handbrake between front seats.
STEERING: Cam and peg.
TYRES: Saloon 5.20 x 13, estate 5.60 x 13.
SUSPENSION: Front independent with coil springs and wishbones, rear semi-elliptic leaf springs, anti-roll bars front and rear, hydraulic shock absorbers.
DIMENSIONS: Length with overriders 12ft 0.25in (3.68m), width 4ft 11.375in (1.51m), height 4ft 8.75in (1.44m), wheelbase 7ft 3.187 (2.21m), track front 3ft 11.375in (1.2m), rear 3ft 11in (1.19m), ground clearance 6in (15.2cm), weight: 948cc model 14cwt 1qtr 14lb (730kg), Countryman 15cwt 0qtr (762kg); 1098cc model 15cwt 1qtr (775.3kg), Countryman 15cwt 3qtr (800.68kg). Note the reduction in length when compared to the mark 1; this was a result of moving the overriders to a different position on the bumpers. Length without

overriders, mark 1 and mark 2 models 12ft 0.25in (3.66m).

CAPACITIES: Fuel 7 gallons (32 litres). Boot 9.25ft³ (0.30m³), Countryman 31ft³ (0.88m³) with rear seat folded.

Gear change diagram.

Austin A55 Cambridge

Introduced in 1959 to replace the Burzi-designed A55, this was the second Farina-styled Austin car to be launched, the first being the smaller A40 in 1958. The first of the medium sized Farina cars was the Wolseley 15/60. The Farina name applied to these cars is derived from the Pininfarina styling house in Italy, which was responsible for the design of the car. The A55 saloon is easily identified from the A60 by its pointed tail fins, a popular styling feature of 1950s cars. However, the MG and Riley models had the shorter, less pronounced tail fins from the start. An A55 estate was launched in 1960, and a point of note is that whilst the A60 saloon had restyled lower tail fins, the A60 estate retained the same large tail fins as on the A55 estate. There was also a

Morris estate but no MG, Riley or Wolseley estates. The A55 was available with a two-tone paint scheme, with the roof, top half of the rear wings, and boot lid painted one colour, and the bonnet and lower half of the car in another. This style was applied to the MG and Riley models, while the Wolseley had the roof and lower half painted one

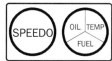

Instrument layout.

Gear change diagram.

colour, and the centre section another, and the Morris had only the roof painted a different colour.

Number produced: 359,325.

Price when introduced: Saloon £879. Standard equipment included water temperature and oil pressure gauges, glove box, parcel shelf, divided front bench seat with individual adjustment for each half, driver's sun visor, rubber mat in front, carpet in rear, and interior bonnet release. In addition, the De Luxe had a heater, passenger sun visor, windscreen washers, fitted carpet in front and rear, armrests on rear doors, overriders and more. Optional equipment for both models included radio, clock, wheel rim embellishers, steering column gear change, and two-tone paintwork.

COLOURS: Single colour: Farina grey, Grampian grey, Sutherland green, Ocean blue, Orchid, Black. Two-tone, lower body first: Farina grey/Horizon blue, Farina grey/Tartan red, Farina grey/Black, Farina grey/Orchid, Orchid/Black.

ENGINE: Four-cylinder, OHV, bore 73.025mm, stroke 88.9mm, 1489cc (90.88in^3), maximum bhp 53 at 4500rpm, SU HS2 carburettor.

GEARBOX: Four-speed, floor-mounted gear change, synchromesh on top three gears, ratios saloon: top 4.55, 3rd 6.25, 2nd 10.08, 1st 16.55, reverse 21.64. Estate: top 4.875, 3rd 6.693, 2nd 10.798, 1st 17.73, reverse 23.181.

REAR AXLE: Hypoid bevel, three-quarter floating, ratio saloon 4.55:1, estate 4.875.

BRAKES: Girling, front and rear 9-inch drums, handbrake between driver's seat and door.

STEERING: Cam and peg.

TYRES: 5.90 x 14. Spare wheel in tray underneath the rear of the car, lowered by unscrewing a bolt located in a readily accessible position inside the boot.

SUSPENSION: Front coil spring and wishbone, rear semi-elliptic leaf springs, front and rear Armstrong hydraulic lever type shock absorbers.

DIMENSIONS: Length with overriders 14ft 10.125in (4.53m), width 5ft 3.5in (1.613m), height 4ft 11.75in (1.518m), wheel base 8ft 3.25in (2.521m), track front 4ft 0.875in (1.241m), rear 4ft 1.875in (1.267m), ground clearance 6.25in (15.9cm), turning circle 37ft 6in (11.43m), weight 1 ton 2qtr 14lb (1050kg).

CAPACITIES: Fuel 10 gallons (45 litres). Boot, saloon: 19ft³ (0.538m³). Estate 51ft³ (1.45m³) with rear seat folded down.

Left, A55; right, A60. Note the different style of indicator lights and position of overriders on bumpers.

The rear boot lid of all saloons had a separate section near the rear screen for the lockable fuel filler flap, care was required when filling up not to spill fuel over the top of the rear wing.

Viewed from the front, the windscreen wipers park to the right on later A55 cars. The earlier Orchid/Black car (on page 35) has wipers parked to the left. The same applies to Morris Oxford, etc.

Austin A60 Cambridge

Introduced in 1961, this was a restyled and upgraded A55 with a larger engine. It was discontinued along with the Riley 4/72 in 1969, the MG Magnette was discontinued in 1968, and the other Farina models, the Morris Oxford and Wolseley 16/60, were discontinued in 1971. The A60 can be easily distinguished from the A55 by its different tail fins, revised front grille, and new front and rear lights. Other changes included completely changing the styling of the two-tone colour scheme to one that was unique to the Cambridge. Both Morris and Wolseley models retained the style introduced with their earlier models. Improvements over the A55 included an enlarged engine of 1622cc, a longer wheelbase, achieved by moving the rear axle backwards, wider front and rear track, and the fitment of front and rear anti-roll bars. Further improvements occurred at various stages throughout its life including the elimination of some greasing points. A lengthened version of the A60 with a six-cylinder 2.4-litre engine – called the Freeway – was produced in both saloon and estate versions in Australia from 1962. A Wolseley version, available only as a saloon

and known as the 24/80, was also produced, but lack of sales led to all these cars being discontinued in 1965. Dimensions were as follows: length 14ft 10in (4.521m), width 5ft 3.5in (1.613m), height 4ft 10in (1.473m). **Number produced:** A60 saloon and estate 276,000 approximately. Some were produced at Longbridge and others at Cowley so accurate figures are unavailable. **Price when introduced:** Saloon £854, Countryman estate £978.

At launch, standard equipment included water temperature and oil pressure gauges, glove box, parcel shelf, divided front bench seat with individual adjustment for each half, driver's sun visor, rubber mat in front, and carpet in rear. De Luxe, in addition to above, had a heater, passenger sun visor, fitted carpet in front and rear, windscreen washers, overriders and more. Optional equipment on both models included radio, clock, wheel rim embellishers, steering column gear change, automatic transmission, and two-tone paint scheme. Later cars also had the option of reclining front seats and a diesel engine.

COLOURS (1962): Single colours: Snowberry white, Farina grey, Grampian grey, Cumulus grey, Horizon blue, Bermuda blue, Persian

blue, Fern green, Embassy maroon, and Black. Two-tone, main body first: Snowberry white/ Embassy maroon, Grampian grey/Cumulus grey, Black/Farina grey. The following all came with Snowberry white side flash: Farina grey, Cumulus grey, Horizon blue, Bermuda blue, Persian blue, Fern green.

Rear lights on the A55 (left), and A60 (right).

ENGINE: Four-cylinder, OHV, bore 76.2mm, stroke 88.9mm, 1622cc (98.94in^3), maximum bhp 61 at 4500rpm, SU HS2 carburettor. Optional diesel, four-cylinder, OHV, bore 77mm, stroke 88.9mm, 1489cc (90.88in^3), maximum bhp 40 at 4000rpm.

GEARBOX: Four-speed, floor-mounted gear change, steering column change optional, synchromesh on top three gears, ratios: top 4.3, 3rd 5.91, 2nd 9.52, 1st 15.64 reverse 20.45. With optional automatic, ratios: top 4.3, 2nd 6.235, 1st 10.277. With diesel engine, ratios: top 4.55, 3rd 6.78, 2nd 10.93, 1st 17.95, reverse 23.47.

REAR AXLE: Hypoid bevel, three-quarter floating, ratio for early cars and diesel model: 4.55:1, automatic and later manual cars: 4.3:1.

BRAKES: Girling, front and rear 9-inch drums, handbrake between driver's seat and door.

STEERING: Cam and peg.

TYRES: 5.90 x 14. Spare wheel in tray underneath the rear of the car.

Instrument layout.

SUSPENSION: Front coil springs and wishbone, rear semi-elliptic leaf springs, front and rear anti-roll bars and telescopic shock absorbers.

DIMENSIONS: Saloon length 14ft 6.5in (4.432m), width 5ft 3.5in (1.613m), height 4ft 10in (1.47m), wheel base 8ft 4.25in (2.546m), track front 4ft 2.625in (1.286m), rear 4ft 3.375in (1.305m), ground clearance 5.875in (15cm), turning circle 37ft (11.278m), weight 1 ton 1cwt 2qtr (1092kg). Estate as saloon except, length 4ft 9.125in (4.52m), and weight 1 ton 3cwt 1qtr (1181kg).

CAPACITIES: Fuel 10 gallons (45 litres). Boot, saloon 19ft^3 (0.538m^3), Countryman estate 51.1ft^3 (1.45m^3) with rear seat folded down.

Foot-operated headlight dipswitch to the left of clutch pedal.

Handbrake by the side of the driver's seat; a common feature on many 1960s cars.

Gear change diagram.

The estate car retained the A55 rear styling.

Austin A99

Introduced in 1959 to replace the A105 Six, there were also Wolseley and Vanden Plas Princess 3-Litre versions of this Farina-designed car. Vanden Plas cars had originally been large upmarket versions of Austin models, and the Vanden Plas name was later applied to some BMC 1100 models, as well as the Allegro. In general appearance, the A99 looked like the A55 which was also introduced in 1959. However, the A99 in A110 guise would be discontinued in 1968, whereas the A60, which was the later version of the A55, would continue until 1969. The engine in the A99 was derived from that used in the Austin-Healey 3000 sports car, an engine which had started life in the Wolseley 6/90 as a 2639cc unit before being used in the Austin-Healey 3000's predecessor, the 100-Six.
Number produced: 15,162.
Price when introduced: £1148.
Standard equipment included water temperature and oil pressure gauges, clock, heater, glove box, parcel shelf, divided

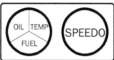

Instrument layout.

Another example of the handbrake beside the driver's seat.

front bench seat with individual adjustment for each half, front and rear seats with leather, opening quarter lights in front and rear doors, two-speed wipers, windscreen washers, overdrive, and overriders. Optional equipment included radio, automatic transmission, and two-tone paint scheme, with a choice of single or two-tone seat and door trim.

COLOURS (1959): Single colour: Horizon blue, Alaskan blue, Farina grey, Grampian grey, Steel grey, Sutherland green, and Black. Two-tone, lower body colour first: Horizon blue/Farina grey, Alaskan blue/Farina grey, Grampian grey/Steel grey, Alaskan blue/Black, and Tartan red/Black.

ENGINE: Six-cylinder, OHV, bore 83.34mm, stroke 88.9mm, 2912cc, (177.63in^3), maximum bhp 112 at 4750rpm, two SU H4 carburettors.

GEARBOX: Three-speed, steering column gear change, Borg-Warner overdrive standard on top and 2nd, all synchromesh gearbox, ratios: o/d top 2.74, top 3.91, o/d 2nd 4.52, 2nd 6.45, 1st 12.10, reverse 11.73, with optional automatic, ratios: top 3.55, 2nd 5.09, 1st 8.19, reverse 7.13.

REAR AXLE: Hypoid bevel, three-quarter floating, ratio 3.9:1, automatic 3.55:1.
BRAKES: Lockheed, power assisted, front 10.75-inch discs, rear 10-inch drums, handbrake between driver's seat and door.
STEERING: Cam and peg.
TYRES: 7.00 x 14, spare wheel in tray underneath the rear of the car, lowered by unscrewing a bolt located in a readily accessible position inside the boot.
SUSPENSION: Front wishbones and coil springs, rear semi-elliptic leaf springs, front and rear anti-roll bars and hydraulic lever type shock absorbers.
DIMENSIONS: Length 15ft 7.5in (4.76m), width 5ft 8.5in (1.74m), height 5ft 0.5in (1.54m), wheelbase 9ft (2.743m), track front 4ft 6in (1.372m), rear 4ft 5.25in (1.352m), ground clearance 6.375in (16.19cm), turning circle 40ft (12.192m), kerb weight 1 ton 11cwt (1574kg).
CAPACITIES: Fuel 16 gallons (73 litres). Boot 18ft^3 (0.51m^3).

Top, A99 front light and grille arrangement, bottom, an A110.

Top, A99 rear light arrangement, bottom, an A110 which has different number plate lights.

Austin A110 mark 1

Introduced in 1961 to replace the A99, changes included a longer wheelbase (achieved by moving the rear axle further back to minimise wheelarch intrusion into the interior), and a floor-mounted gear change. This, however, now limited the car's ability to seat three in the front, even though it had retained the bench seat as used in the A99. Externally, a new radiator grille and side light/indicator arrangement distinguished it from the A99. There were no changes to the rear lights or tail fins as there had been with the A55 and A60 models. The spare wheel remained under the boot floor in a separate carrier that could be lowered without moving any luggage, which also meant that there was no need to put a wet or muddy wheel into the boot in the event of a puncture. The handbrake was on the right of the driver's seat, a feature used by other manufacturers – such as Rootes – during the 1960s. Many cars, however, continued to appear with the handbrake underneath the dashboard, as it was frequently found on many cars of the 1950s – including the Austin A70 and

A105. This under-the-dashboard location was reintroduced on the Austin 1800. It was not until the 1970s that a centrally placed handbrake between the front seats became universally adopted, and then from around 2010 onwards the handbrake lever started to disappear on some cars, replaced by a button that electronically controlled the handbrake, a feature that leaves no way of stopping a car in an emergency if the main braking system develops a fault.
Number produced: 12,200 approximately.
Price when introduced: £1270.

ENGINE: Six-cylinder, OHV, bore 83.34mm, stroke 88.9mm, 2912cc (177.63in^3), maximum bhp 120 at 4750rpm, two SU H4 carburettors.

GEARBOX: Three-speed all synchromesh gearbox, floor-mounted gear change, Borg-Warner overdrive, standard on top and second, ratios: o/d top 3.00, top 3.91, o/d 2nd 4.95, 2nd 6.45, 1st 12.07, reverse 11.73.

REAR AXLE: Hypoid bevel, three-quarter floating, ratio manual 3.91:1.

BRAKES: Lockheed, power assisted front 10-inch discs, rear 10-inch drums.

STEERING: Cam and lever.

TYRES: 7.00 x 14.

SUSPENSION: Front wishbones and coil springs, rear semi-elliptic leaf springs, front and rear anti-roll bars and lever type shock absorbers.

DIMENSIONS: Length 15ft 8in (4.775m), width 5ft 8.5in (1.74m), height 5ft 0in

Instrument layout.

Manual gear change diagram.

(1.524m), wheel base 9ft 2in (2.79m), track front 4ft 5.8125in (1.366m), rear 4ft 5.25in (1.352m), ground clearance 6.25in (15.875cm), turning circle 41ft (12.5m), weight 1 ton 10cwt 2qtr (1575kg).
CAPACITIES: Fuel 16 gallons (73 litres). Boot 18ft^3 (0.51m^3).

Austin A110 mark 2

The mark 2 was introduced in 1964 as a De Luxe or Super De Luxe saloon. It had a four-speed gearbox, but overdrive became an optional extra. Other changes included smaller wheels (now 13-inch instead of 14-inch), thicker front brake discs, increased length rear leaf springs with twin telescopic shock absorbers and no anti-roll bar. The front suspension received new type shock absorbers but retained the anti-roll bar. Greasing points were now eliminated from the steering column, the dashboard was changed to a rectangular, or, as it was often called, ribbon style, as used in the 1800 mark 1, which was also introduced in 1964. The front seats were raised and the Super Deluxe had reclining front seats, rear door map pockets, and other additional equipment. The A110 mark 2 was discontinued in March 1968, replaced by the new Austin 3-Litre which had been introduced at the 1967 Motor Show. However, although the 3-Litre resembled a large 1800 'Landcrab,' it continued the

trend of traditional rear-wheel drive. Plans for Wolseley and Vanden Plas models were considered, but with BMC having acquired Jaguar, and the merger with British Leyland imminent, perhaps there were already enough models to fill the luxury end of the market; no Wolseley or Vanden Plas variants of the 3-Litre were ever made.
Number produced: 13,300 approximately. This was less than the A99, which had been produced for a shorter period.
Price in 1965: £998 to £1210, dependent on model.
Standard equipment included heater, fuel, water temperature and oil pressure gauges in three-in-one instrument display, single speed wipers, windscreen washers, driver's sun visor, glove box, divided front bench

seat with individual adjustment for each seat, and interior bonnet release. Super De Luxe, with different instrument arrangement, also had an ammeter, clock, two-speed wipers, headlight flasher, passenger sun visor, cigar lighter, armrests, map pockets, veneered dash and door cappings, reclining

AMP	CLOCK	OIL	TEMP	SPEEDO	FUEL

Instrument layout diagram for Super De Luxe.

front seats with folding picnic table in back of each seat, leather upholstery, carpeted boot, and overriders. Optional equipment for all models included radio, overdrive, Borg-Warner 35 automatic transmission, Hydrosteer power assisted steering, Normalair air-conditioning (on the Super De Luxe only), and two-tone paint scheme, and for the De Luxe saloon, electric clock and passenger sun visor.

COLOURS: Single colours: Titan beige, Connaught green, Grampian grey, Maroon, Black, Steel grey, and Blue Royale. Two-tones (Super De Luxe only), upper body colour first: Canyon grey/Stone, Titan beige/Stone, Almond green/Connaught green, Alaskan blue/Blue Royale, Persian blue/Alaskan blue.
ENGINE: As A110 mark 1.
GEARBOX: Four-speed, floor-mounted gear change, overdrive optional, synchromesh on top three gears, ratios: top 3.91, 3rd 5.11, 2nd 8.10, 1st 10.31, reverse 13.26, with optional automatic, ratios: top 3.55, 2nd 5.15, 1st 8.48, reverse 7.42.
REAR AXLE: Hypoid bevel, three-quarter floating, ratios manual 3.91:1, automatic 3.55:1.
BRAKES: Lockheed, power assisted with pressure limiting valve fitted to apportion

more accurate braking between front and rear wheels, to reduce the risk of skidding whilst braking. Note: this should not to be confused with the more sophisticated anti-lock braking systems fitted to modern cars. Front 10-inch discs, rear 10-inch drums.

STEERING: Cam and lever, power assistance optional.

TYRES: 7.50 x 13.

SUSPENSION: Front coil springs, telescopic shock absorbers and anti-roll bar, rear semi-elliptic leaf springs and twin telescopic shock absorbers.

DIMENSIONS: Length 15ft 8in (4.775m), width 5ft 8.5in (1.74m), height 5ft 0in (1.524m), wheel base 9ft 2in (2.79m), track front 4ft 7in (1.397m), rear 4ft 5.25in (1.352m), ground clearance 6.5in (16.51cm), turning circle 41ft (12.5m), weight dependent on model 1 ton 11cwt (1575kg) approximately.

CAPACITIES: Fuel 16 gallons (73 litres). Boot 18ft^3 (0.51m^3).

Manual gear change diagram.

Automatic gear change diagram.

Austin Seven and Mini

Introduced in August 1959 alongside its Morris counterpart, the Mini-Minor, this car is thought by many to have been the car that introduced front-wheel drive to the motoring masses. It was actually the Citroën Traction Avant that took on this role 25 years earlier in 1934. However, the 'Mini' had the longer production run, and was ultimately produced in greater numbers.

Designed by Sir Alec Issigonis at a time when people were buying bubble cars in the wake of the so-called Suez crisis (when supplies of oil were cut off and fuel rationing was introduced), the Mini, as it would later become known, was advertised as "Wizardry on Wheels." Issigonis had worked for Morris Motors for a number of years, and had designed another legendary car – the Morris Minor, which was launched in 1948 – but he left shortly after the Nuffield Organisation (which Morris was a part of) merged with the Austin Motor Company to form the British Motor Corporation (BMC). He worked for a few years for Alvis motors returning in 1956 to BMC. The design brief was to produce a car capable of carrying four people, and in order to maximise interior space, the decision was made to produce a front-wheel drive car, thus eliminating the need for a transmission tunnel running through the centre of the vehicle carrying the prop shaft. By mounting the gearbox underneath the engine, which was mounted transversely, the overall size could be kept to a minimum. 10-inch wheels minimised

Cars this page and next are Austin Seven.

rear wheelarch intrusion, and with storage space inside the car maximised using a full-width front parcel shelf, space under the rear seats, and door bins, the boot did not need to be large. A novel feature was the rear number plate being hinged, so that it hung down when the boot lid was left open to increase luggage capacity. Other innovations included the use of sub frames for the engine and suspension, and instead of conventional steel springs, rubber cone suspension – comprised of inner and outer cones, with rubber inserted between them, which compressed when the car ran over uneven surfaces – was fitted, one to each side at the front and rear of the car. Unfortunately, the small wheels could cause the suspension to feel hard, but it made for better handling than cars fitted with softer suspension, which could cause a wallowing effect.

From an early start, the Mini proved a popular choice for motor racing, ultimately leading to the development of the Mini Cooper. Hydrolastic suspension was introduced in 1964, and comprised of cylinders containing a fluid which was

compressed when the car hit a bump, absorbing the impact and causing the fluid to flow, via the interconnected front and rear pipework, to the rear of the car ready for the rear wheels to encounter the bump. In 1969, the suspension reverted to the original rubber cone type following some issues with the Hydrolastic system, such as the front end of the car lifting when the boot was filled with heavy objects. Some cars also developed leaks in the system as they aged. Some models, such as the Countryman estate, vans and pickups, were never fitted with Hydrolastic suspension. Although much loved by many, the Mini encountered a number of problems early on in its life, including water leaks into the interior, with the ignition system suffering from water coming straight through the front grille, as the radiator had been fitted to the side. This was subsequently rectified by fitting a plastic cover over the sparkplug leads.

The model range at launch consisted of Basic and De Luxe models. An estate joined the range in 1960. In 1961, the first Mini Cooper appeared, and a Super model was

also introduced. In 1962, the Austin Seven became the Austin Mini, and a Super De Luxe replaced both the De Luxe and Super models. At this time, changes were also made to the gearbox. The Super De Luxe became the De Luxe in 1964, when the Hydrolastic suspension was introduced. There were further changes to the gearbox, a new clutch, front brakes were improved, and a key operated starter switch replaced the floor-mounted button. In 1965, automatic transmission became available as an option.

Number produced: 520,000 approximately (Austin Seven and Mini mark 1).

Price in 1959: Basic saloon £497, De Luxe £537.

Price in 1962: Basic £448, De Luxe £535, Super £558, Countryman £551.

Standard equipment for the 1962 Basic saloon models included large front door bins, cubby box with ashtray either side of rear seat, and cloth trimmed seats. De Luxe models had a heater, windscreen washers, passenger sun visor, opening rear quarter lights, vinyl treated fabric trim, vinyl covered dashboard, door kick plates, bumper

overriders, wheel trims and bright finish for sills and windows, and chrome-plated petrol cap and rear number plate surround. Super, in addition to De Luxe features, had water temperature and oil pressure gauges, a roof-mounted interior light, chromed lever type interior door handles instead of pull strings, overriders with 'nudge bars,' stainless steel window surrounds and sill finishers, two-tone paint scheme with roof in white or black, and front grille with vertical bars, in addition to the horizontal wavy bars of the Basic and De Luxe. Optional equipment

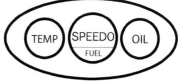

Left, Basic and De Luxe Mini. Below, Super and Mini Cooper dashboard layout.

included radio, and wing mirrors (standard on Countryman). For the 1962 Super De Luxe, the interior door handles were replaced by the pull cord type of door opener, the front ashtrays gained lids, and the front grille was changed.

COLOURS (1959): Tartan red, Speedwell blue, Farina grey.
ENGINE: Four-cylinder, OHV, bore 62.94mm, stroke 68.26mm, 848cc ($51.8in^3$), maximum bhp 34 at 5500rpm, SU HS2 carburettor.
GEARBOX: Four-speed, floor-mounted gear change, synchromesh on top three gears, ratios: top 3.765, 3rd 5.316, 2nd 8.178, 1st 13.659, reverse 13.659. Front-wheel drive with helical spur gears and open driveshafts with universal joints, final drive ratio 3.765:1.
BRAKES: Lockheed front and rear 7-inch drums with handbrake between the front seats.
STEERING: Rack and pinion.
TYRES: 5.20 x 10.
SUSPENSION: Front independent wishbone, rear independent trailing arms, with Moulton rubber cone springs and Armstrong telescopic shock absorbers front and rear.
DIMENSIONS: Length saloon, 10ft 0.25in (3.05m), width 4ft 7.5in (1.41m), height saloon 4ft 5in (1.346m), wheel base saloon 6ft 8in (2.03m), estate 7ft 0.25in (2.14m), track front 3ft 11.325in (1.203m), rear 3ft 9.875in (1.165m), ground clearance 6.125in (1.56cm), turning circle 31ft 7in (9.63m), unladen weight 12cwt 1qtr 8lb (626.38kg). Estate as saloon except, length 10ft 9.9in (3.29m), wheelbase 7ft 0.25in (2.14m).
CAPACITIES: Fuel 5.5 gallons (25 litres). Boot saloon $6ft^3$ ($1.7m^3$), estate $18.5ft^3$ ($0.52m^3$) or $35.5ft^3$ ($1.01m^3$) with rear seat folded down.

Gear change diagram.

This is an Austin Mini, not a Seven.

Austin Mini Cooper and Cooper S

Introduced in 1961, it used the A-series engine, but with a longer stroke and reduced bore. Additional differences over the other models in the range included two carburettors, front disc brakes, remote control gear change, and a different front grille, but most striking of all had to be the two-tone paint scheme with the roof being painted in either black or white, according to the main body colour. Initially referred to as the Austin Seven Cooper, within months it had become the Austin Mini Cooper, and was fitted with a 16-blade radiator fan, in place of the original four. In 1963, an additional Cooper model the 'S' was introduced. This retained the same stroke as the original standard cars, but had an enlarged bore producing a 1071cc engine. Further changes from the 997cc Cooper included larger disc brakes, which were now power assisted, wider front and rear track, and radial, instead of crossply, tyres. At the beginning of 1964, a 998cc engine, which had been introduced with the Riley Elf and Wolseley Hornet mark 2 models, replaced the original 997cc Cooper unit. This new engine had a shorter stroke and wider bore, and the Cooper version was once again fitted with twin carburettors. In April 1964, the 1071cc Cooper S was replaced by two new models with 970cc and 1275cc engines. The 1275cc engine would eventually become the sole Mini Cooper engine. The last of the original Mini Cooper series of cars, the 1275 S, was discontinued in 1971. After this, the Mini Clubman 1275 GT, which had been introduced in 1969 and had replaced the standard Mini Cooper, took over the role as the sole performance model, until all Clubman models were phased out with the introduction of the Metro in 1980. The Mini Cooper name would, however, reappear in 1990 as part of a range of special edition models, and it marked the return of the 1275cc engine to the Mini. The Cooper name then disappeared again when all Minis were discontinued in 2000.
Number produced: Approximately 40,000 Austin Coopers, and 12,000 Austin Cooper S models were produced by 1970.

Above: Austin Cooper S.

Details of Austin Cooper models with differences from standard 848cc Mini as follows:

997 model: September 1961 to 1964
Instruments as Super model, 16-blade cooling fan from late 1961.
ENGINE: Bore 62.43mm, stroke 81.28mm, 997cc (60.86in^3), maximum bhp 55 at 6000rpm, two SU HS2 carburettors.
GEARBOX: Floor-mounted remote control gear change lever, ratios: top 3.765, 3rd 5.11, 2nd 7.21, 1st 12.05, reverse 12.05. Final drive ratio 3.765 with the option of 3.44:1 (see 1071 model).
BRAKES: Front 7-inch discs, rear 7-inch drums.
DIMENSIONS: Front track 3ft 11.75in (1.213m), weight 12cwt 2qtr (636kg).

998 model: January 1964 to 1969
Note: mark 2 model introduced in October 1967 had new rear lights, enlarged rear window, and revised shape front grille.
ENGINE: Bore 64.6mm, stroke 76.2mm, 998cc (60.86in^3), maximum bhp 55 at 5800rpm, two SU HS2 carburettors.
GEARBOX: As 997 model but with new type diaphragm clutch from September 1964, and all synchromesh gearbox from late 1968.
TYRES: 145 x 10 radial ply.

SUSPENSION: Early cars, rubber cone type, then from September 1964, front independent wishbone, rear trailing arms with interconnected Hydrolastic displacers front and rear.
DIMENSIONS: As 997 model.

1071 S: April 1963 to September 1964
Equipment as Cooper 997, except ventilated wheels, additional 5.5-gallon fuel tank, oil cooler, and sumpguard.
ENGINE: Bore 70.64mm, stroke 68.26mm, 1071cc (65.3in^3), maximum bhp 70 at 6000rpm, two SU HS2 carburettors.
GEARBOX: Floor-mounted remote control gearlever, standard ratios as Cooper 997 with 3.765 final drive. With optional 3.44 final drive, ratios: top 3.44, 3rd 4.66, 2nd 6.59, 1st 11.0, reverse 11.0. A close ratio gearbox was also available.
BRAKES: Front 7.5-inch discs, rear 7-inch drums, power assisted.
DIMENSIONS: Front track 4ft 0.4in (1.229m), rear 3ft 10.9in (1.191m), weight 12cwt 2qtr 10lb (640kg).

970 S: April 1964 to January 1965
ENGINE: Bore 70.64mm, stroke 61.91mm, 970cc (59.21in^3), maximum bhp 65 at 6500rpm, two SU HS2 carburettors.
SUSPENSION: Rubber cone initially, then Hydrolastic from September 1964.

1275 S: April 1964 to July 1971
Twin fuel tanks became standard in 1966, along with modifications to the suspension. Note: mark 2 model introduced in October 1967 had new rear lights, enlarged rear window and revised shape front grille. The mark 3, introduced in March 1970, featured concealed door hinges and wind-up windows but was no longer offered with two-tone paint scheme.
ENGINE: Bore 70.64mm, stroke 81.33mm, 1275cc (77.8in^3), maximum bhp 76 at 5800rpm, two SU HS2 carburettors.
GEARBOX: Four-speed, synchromesh on top three gears, ratios as 1071 S, all synchromesh gearbox from 1968.
DIMENSIONS: Front track 3ft 11.53in (1.207m), rear 3ft 10.31in (1.176m), weight 13cwt 2qtr 23lb (698kg).
CAPACITIES: (from 1966) Fuel 11 gallons (50 litres). Boot 4ft^3 (0.11m^3)

Austin Mini mark 2

Introduced in October 1967 with a new front grille extending further across the front of the car, and losing its original curved shape. Also new were a larger rear window and lights, but the exposed door hinges and sliding windows remained. An additional engine of 998cc was introduced with remote control gear change. Revised rack and pinion steering reduced the turning circle from 32ft to 28ft, front brakes had two leading shoes, the rear retained leading and trailing shoes, and the new indicator stalk incorporated headlamp flasher and dipswitch. The Countryman estate was unchanged from the mark 1 at the rear, but gained the new front grille and was only available with the 998cc engine. The car range now comprised Austin 850, 850 Super De Luxe, 1000 Super De Luxe, and Countryman. There were Morris versions of all the above, as well as 850 and 1000 vans and pickups. During 1968, internal door handles replaced the original pull cords and all synchromesh gear boxes were introduced.
Number produced: 176,500 approximately. Optional extras included seatbelts, automatic transmission, reclining front seats, and heated rear window.

ENGINE: Four-cylinder, OHV, bore 64.58mm, stroke 76.2mm, 998cc (60.89in^3), maximum bhp 38 at 5250rpm, SU HS4 carburettor. For 848cc engine see Mini mark 1. Note: the

Above: Manual gear change diagram.
Right: Automatic.

998cc engine was derived from the 1098cc engine used in the Austin 1100 models; it was not developed from the 848cc engine.

GEARBOX: Four-speed, floor-mounted gear change, synchromesh on top three gears, ratios: top 3.44, 3rd 4.86, 2nd 7.47, 1st 12.48, reverse 12.48. Front-wheel drive with helical spur gears and open driveshafts with universal joints, final drive ratio 3.44:1. Note: 848cc engine retained the original mark 1 ratios.

BRAKES/STEERING/TYRES: As Mini mark 1.

SUSPENSION: Initially, front independent wishbone, rear trailing arms with interconnected front and rear Hydrolastic displacers. From 1969, reverted to rubber cone type.

DIMENSIONS: Generally as Mini mark 1 except turning circle now 28ft 6in (8.6m).

Mini mark 3

Introduced in October 1969, the Austin and Morris names disappeared, and the Wolseley Hornet and Riley Elf were discontinued, with the Mini effectively becoming a marque in its own right. Badges consisted of a small bonnet badge with 'Mini' on it, a rear boot badge denoting the engine size, and British Leyland badges on each side of the car just ahead of the doors. Although it appeared to have the same bodyshell as the mark 2, there were changes made to accommodate the new doors with hidden hinges, and wind-down front windows. The model range now consisted of 850 and 1000 saloons; the estate was replaced by the new Mini Clubman estate. Suspension was the original rubber cone type, and

would remain so for the rest of the Mini's life. The Clubman saloon, however, had Hydrolastic suspension initially. Changes to the Mini were frequent between 1969 and 1979, and included radial ply tyres, inertia reel seatbelts, and heated rear window and door mirrors, which all became standard equipment on both models. New for 1969 were restyled seats and trim, twin column-mounted stalks controlling lights and windscreen wipers, rocker switches replaced toggle type, a combined ignition/steering lock, revised suspension and more. The 1000 model also gained reclining front seats and reversing lights. It was during this time that special editions of the Mini started to appear, including the 1100 Special to celebrate twenty years of Mini production. It was fitted with the 1098cc engine from the Mini Clubman, alloy wheels with matt black wheelarch extensions, extra indicators on the front wings, and was only available with Silver or Rose metallic paint.

Prices: when introduced, 850 £596, 1000 £675. Prices increased in 1974 (following the introduction of VAT and Car Tax to replace Purchase Tax) to 850 £1099, 1000 £1184, and by 1979 an 850 cost £2157 and 1000 £2278.

Standard equipment at launch: the 850 model continued the tradition of providing minimal equipment at the bottom of the range, retaining the centrally-mounted speedometer and fuel gauge, and fixed non-opening rear quarter windows. The 1000 model got water temperature and oil pressure gauges, fresh air heater, passenger sun visor, and hinged rear quarter windows. Optional equipment for both models included, seatbelts, rake adjustable front seats, heated rear window, and radial ply tyres. For the 1000 saloon only, automatic transmission, overriders and more.

COLOURS (1972): Glacier white, Blaze, Flame red, Teal blue, Aqua, Black Tulip, Green Mallard, Harvest gold, Limeflower, Bronze yellow.

ENGINE: As Mini mark 1 and 2, but note 848cc engine had SU HS4 carburettor from 1974.

GEARBOX: Four-speed, floor-mounted gear change, all synchromesh. 850 ratios: top 3.76, 3rd 5.39, 2nd 8.34, 1st 13.25, reverse 13.33. 1000 ratios: top 3.44, 3rd 4.93, 2nd 7.63, 1st 12.13, reverse 12.19. Front-wheel drive as Mini mark 2, final drive ratio, 850 model: 3.76:1. 1000 model: 3.44:1.

BRAKES/STEERING: As Mini mark 1.

TYRES: 5.20 x 10 crossply, later models 145 x 10 radial ply.

SUSPENSION: Front independent wishbone, rear independent trailing arms, rubber cone springs and telescopic shock absorbers front and rear.

DIMENSIONS: Length 10ft 0.25in (3.05m), width 4ft 7.5in (1.41m), height 4ft 5in (1.346m), wheel base 6ft 8in (2.03m), track front 3ft 11.8in (1.241m), rear 3ft 10.4in (1.179m), ground clearance 6.125in (1.56cm), turning circle 28ft 6in (8.6m), weight, 850 model: 12cwt 0qtr 16lb (617kg), 1000 model: 12cwt 1qtr 3lb (625kg).

CAPACITIES: As Mini mark 1.

The car above is an Innocenti.

Mini Clubman

Introduced in October 1969, the Clubman was an attempt at revising the Mini range. The 1275 GT replaced the Mini Cooper, and the estate, with its fake wood trim reminiscent of 1950s estate cars, replaced the Mini Countryman and remained in production for a while after the Metro had replaced the Clubman saloons in 1980. Later estates had stripes along the sides, and all Clubmans received revised front grilles in 1976. The Clubman had a different interior to the standard Mini; a rectangular pod in front of the driver contained two or three instruments dependent on model, face level ventilation and contoured seats were standard. Changes to the Clubman models were generally of a mechanical, rather than cosmetic, type with the saloon switching from Hydrolastic to rubber cone suspension

This car has been fitted with a fabric sunroof.

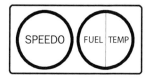

Above, Clubman saloon and estate instrument layout.

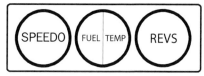

1275 GT instrument layout.

in 1971; the estate had rubber cone suspension from the start. All 1973 models had an alternator and radial ply tyres, and a driver's door mirror replaced the twin wing mirrors on estates. With the exception of automatic models, a 1098cc engine replaced the original 998cc engine in 1975, and a heated rear window and tinted glass for saloons, inertia reel seatbelts, reclining front seats, twin column-mounted stalks for lights and wipers, hazard warning lights, ignition/steering lock, revised suspension, and reversing lights had all been added by the end of 1977.

Price in 1970: Saloon £771, GT £894, estate £830.

Standard equipment included fuel and water temperature gauges, heater, and all synchromesh gearbox. GT adds revolution counter, power assisted brakes, Rostyle wheels with radial ply tyres, and 1275cc engine. Optional extras were heated rear window (saloons), rake adjustable front seats, and automatic transmission (not GT).

COLOURS (1976): Glacier white, Tahiti blue, Damask red, Flamenco, Sand Glow, Antique gold.

1969 specification
ENGINE: Four-cylinder, OHV, 998cc as Mini

mark 2 except SU HS2 carburettor, (automatic SU HS4). Later cars, bore 64.58mm, stroke 83.73mm, 1098cc (67.02in³), maximum bhp 45 at 5250rpm, SU HS4 carburettor. GT model, bore 70.64mm, stroke 81.33mm, 1275cc (77.8in³), maximum bhp 60 at 5250rpm, SU HS4 carburettor.

GEARBOX: GT model, four-speed, all synchromesh, ratios: top 3.65, 3rd 5.22, 2nd 8.10, 1st 12.87, reverse 12.23. Final drive ratio 3.65:1. Clubman saloon and estate models see below.

1971 specification

GEARBOX: Four-speed, all synchromesh, remote control floor-mounted gearlever, ratios: saloon and estate, top 3.44, 3rd 4.93, 2nd 7.63, 1st 12.13, reverse 12.19. GT, top 3.44, 3rd 4.64, 2nd 7.19, 1st 11.35, reverse 11.52. Front-wheel drive as Mini mark 1, final drive ratio all models 3.44:1.

BRAKES: Front and rear 7-inch drums, GT front 7.5-inch discs, rear 7-inch drums, power assisted. GT models with 12-inch wheels had 8.4-inch front discs, non power assisted. All later models of Clubman had dual circuit brake system.

STEERING: Rack and pinion.

TYRES: Saloon and estate 5.20 x 10, later cars and early GT 145 x 10, GT from 1974 onwards 155 x 12.

SUSPENSION: Saloon and GT Hydrolastic until 1971 then rubber cone. Estates had rubber cone type suspension from introduction.

DIMENSIONS: Saloon length 10ft 4.64in (3.17m), width 4ft 7.5in (1.41m), height 4ft 5in (1.34m), wheelbase saloons 6ft 8.2in (2.036m), track front 4ft 0in (1.219m), rear 3ft 11.25in (1.2m), weight 12cwt 2qtr 6lb (639kg). GT weight 13cwt 0qtr 20lb (670kg). Estate as saloon except, length 11ft 1.92in (3.4m), height 4ft 5.5in (1.36m), wheelbase 7ft 0.2in (2.139m), weight 13cwt 2qtr 2lb (687kg).

CAPACITIES: Fuel, saloons 5.5 gallons (25 litres), estate 6.5 gallons (29.5 litres). From 1976, saloons 7.5 gallons (29.5 litres). Boot saloons 5.5ft³ (0.16m³), estate 18.5ft³ (0.52m³) or 35.3ft³ (1m³) with rear seat folded down. From 1976, saloons 4.1ft³ (0.116m³).

Mini City, Super and Mayfair

In 1979 the Mini range was revised to include two 850 models (the City and Super Deluxe) and the 1000 became the Super. In 1980, all models were fitted with a larger fuel tank of 7.5 gallons, which effectively reduced the size of the boot. Almost immediately after this, the range was revised again. Gone were the 848cc engine models, the City, which was the bottom of the range, now had a 998cc engine, and the 1000 Super became the HL, with the double gauge instrument pod from the Metro replacing the central instrument display that had been a feature of the Mini since its introduction in 1959. In 1982, the range was renamed again as City E and HLE, and within a few months the HLE became the Mayfair. The Mini Sprite and Mini 25 special editions followed shortly after, and in 1984 the 12-inch wheels, wheelarch spats, and front disc brakes from the Mini 25 model were fitted as standard to City E and Mayfair models. In quick succession, from 1985 onwards, other special editions were rolled out: Ritz (Silver), Chelsea (Red), Piccadilly (Gold), Park Lane (Black), followed by Advantage (white with tennis net graphics on the side), Red Hot, Jet Black, and then Rose and Sky (white with pink and pale blue coloured roofs), and Flame and Racing (red and green with white roofs). The Mini Thirty followed in 1989, and soon other cars with a checker board or Union Jack roof could be seen everywhere. Standard equipment on the (1982) City E included twin sun visors with passenger vanity mirror, full-width trimmed and padded parcel shelf, heater, driver's door mirror, inertia reel front seatbelts, two-speed wipers with flick wipe, electric screen washers, heated rear window, hazard warning lights, reversing lights, and rear foglight. Mayfair adds water temperature gauge, radio, reclining front seats, tinted glass, passenger door mirror, front door pockets, locking fuel cap and more. Optional extras included automatic transmission, black or metallic paint finish, alloy wheels, and wheelarch extensions. For 1983, the Mayfair gained adjustable headrests, and for 1987, the City E had the

two-pack instrument panel with fuel and water temperature gauges, while the Mayfair now had a triple-pack instrument panel featuring a tachometer (revolution counter). For both models, wheelarch extensions, door handles, bumpers, and grille were Nimbus grey. 1988 changes included front seat headrests for the City, the E was no longer included in the name, and the Mayfair had a radio/cassette player in place of the radio.

COLOURS (1983): Arum white, Cinnabar red, Primula yellow, Clove brown, Eclipse blue, and Black. Metallics were Silver leaf, Opaline green, and Zircon blue.

COLOURS (1985): Arum white, Targa red, Champagne beige, Primula yellow, Clove brown, Eclipse blue, and Black. Metallics were Silver leaf, Cashmere gold, Oporto red, Opaline green, Zircon blue, Moonraker blue.

COLOURS (1988): White diamond, Flame red, Oyster beige, Solar yellow, Henley blue, and Black. Metallics were Pulsar silver, Atlantic blue, and, for the Mayfair only, Steel grey,

Stone grey, Mulberry red, British Racing green, Azure blue.

1985 specification

ENGINE: Four-cylinder, OHV, bore 64.58mm, stroke 76.2mm, 998cc (60.89in^3), maximum bhp 40 at 5000rpm, SU HS4 carburettor, catalytic converter optional from 1989.

GEARBOX: Four-speed, floor-mounted gear change, synchromesh on all gears, ratios: top 3.105, 3rd 4.42, 2nd 6.78, 1st 11.32, reverse 11.39. Front-wheel drive as Mini mark 2, final drive ratio 3.105:1.

BRAKES: Dual circuit, front 8.4-inch discs, rear 7-inch drums, power assisted from 1988.

TYRES: 145/70 x 12.

STEERING: Rack and pinion.

SUSPENSION: Rubber cone type.

DIMENSIONS: Length 10ft 0.25in, width with door mirror(s), City 4ft 9.4in (1.46m), Mayfair 5ft 1.3in (1.56m), height 4ft 5.25in (1.35m), wheel base 6ft 8in (2.03m), track front 4ft 0.78in (1.24m), rear 3ft 11.44in (1.2m), ground clearance 5.75in (147cm), kerb weight according to model 12cwt 1qtr 10lb (625kg) to 13cwt 1qtr 1lb (675kg).

CAPACITIES: Fuel 7.5 gallons (34 litres). Boot 4.1ft^3 (0.12m^3).

Mini 1990 onwards

1990 saw the reintroduction of the Cooper name, and a 1275cc engine, like that previously used in the Clubman GT, was fitted. In 1992, the City and Mayfair with 998cc engines were replaced by Sprite and Mayfair models with 1275cc engines. The Sprite generally had the same equipment as the City model it replaced. For 1993, all cars received an internal bonnet release, and the Mayfair a walnut dashboard. 1994 saw single point fuel-injection replace the SU carburettor in the Sprite and Mayfair, and in 1995 rear seat inertia reel seatbelts and a remote controlled alarm/immobiliser

Above: A Rio. Below: A Sprite.

became standard equipment. The Cooper had been fitted with fuel-injection from 1991, as was the cabriolet, a completely new model with a special bodykit featuring extra wide wheelarch extensions and special bumpers. Special editions regularly appeared throughout the 1990s, with specification changes continuing until 1996, at which point the dashboard was completely restyled, an airbag fitted in the steering wheel, and safety beams inserted in the doors. After this, only cosmetic changes were made until 2000, when the Mini was discontinued, by which time over five million of all-types had been built.

COLOURS (1992): Cooper 1.3i: White diamond, Storm grey, and Quicksilver, all with black roof. Flame red, Black, and British

Racing green, all with white roof. Mayfair model: White diamond, Flame red, Black, Midnight blue, and metallics were British Racing green, Storm grey, Pearlescent Nightfire red, and Pearlescent Caribbean blue. Sprite, in addition to Mayfair colours: Cranberry red, Henley blue, and metallics were Nordic blue, Amethyst, and Quicksilver.

1992 specification

ENGINE: Four-cylinder, OHV, bore 70.6mm, stroke 81.3mm, 1275cc (77.8in³), Cooper maximum bhp 63 at 5700rpm, single point fuel-injection. Sprite and Mayfair maximum bhp 50 at 5000rpm, SU carburettor. All cars fitted with catalytic converter as standard.
BRAKES/TYRES/STEERING/SUSPENSION: see 1985 City and Mayfair models.

Top left: A Mayfair. Top right: A 1275. Bottom: A Cooper Sport.

Austin 1100 mark 1

Introduced in September 1963, almost a year after its Morris and MG counterparts, but two years ahead of the Riley and Wolseley versions, the Austin 1100 used the Hydrolastic suspension system developed by Alex Moulton, which consisted of interconnected front and rear displacer units on each side, which, when a wheel passes over an uneven surface, causes rubber cups in the unit to come together squeezing fluid along pipes to the opposite end of the car, keeping the car level, and eliminating the bounce effect associated with conventional springs. Two versions of the car were available, Basic and De Luxe saloons, both with four doors. A two-door estate was introduced in March 1966. It had a folding rear seat, which, together with the optional reclining front seats, meant that, according to brochures, a double bed could be formed. Probably more useful was that, with the front passenger seat folded down, it provided an extremely useful load length. In both the saloon and estate, the spare wheel was under a panel in the boot, requiring all luggage to be removed to access it, but unlike the Mini, the battery was under the bonnet with the engine. In 1965, automatic transmission became available, and a heater became standard equipment on the De Luxe model.

Standard equipment at launch included water temperature gauge, driver's sun visor, windscreen washers, and front wheel disc brakes. De Luxe adds passenger sun visor, front door bins, overriders, and stainless steel window frames on doors. Optional equipment included heater, seatbelts, leather trimmed seats, locking petrol cap, bonnet lock, and anti-mist rear window panel, a popular accessory before heated rear windows became available.

COLOURS: Saloon: Tartan red, Connaught green, Honolulu blue, Alaskan blue, Arabian grey, and Laguna beige. Countryman estate: Trafalgar blue, and Cumulus grey. All models: Maroon, El Paso beige, Black.

Instrument layout.

Gear change diagram.

ENGINE: Four-cylinder, OHV, bore 64.58mm, stroke 83.72mm, 1098cc (67.02in^3), maximum bhp 48 at 5100rpm, SU HS2 carburettor.
GEARBOX: Four-speed, floor-mounted gear change, synchromesh on top three gears, ratios: top 4.133, 3rd 5.83, 2nd 8.97, 1st 15.00, reverse 15.00. Front-wheel drive with helical spur gears and open driveshafts with universal joints, final drive ratio 4.133:1.
BRAKES: Lockheed with pressure limiting valve fitted to apportion more accurate braking between front and rear wheels, front 8-inch discs, rear 8-inch drums.
STEERING: Rack and pinion.
TYRES: 5.50 x 12.
SUSPENSION: Front independent wishbone, rear independent trailing arms and anti-roll bar, front and rear interconnected Hydrolastic displacers.
DIMENSIONS: Length (with overriders) 12ft 2.75in (3.73m), width 5ft 0.4in (1.534m), height 4ft 5in (1.35m), wheel base 7ft 9.5in (2.375m), track front 4ft 3.5in (1.308m), rear 4ft 2.9in (1.292m), ground clearance 6.125in (15.6cm), turning circle 34ft (10.363m), kerb weight saloon, 16cwt 1qtr 9lb (830kg)
CAPACITIES: Fuel tank 8 gallons (36.37 litres). Boot, saloon 9.5ft^3 (0.269m^3), estate 14ft^3 (0.4m^3) or 37.7ft^3 (1.07m^3) with rear seat folded down.

Austin 1100 mark 2/1300

The 1100 mark 2 and 1300, with revised rear light arrangement and indicator repeater flashers on the front wings, were introduced in October 1967. The front grilles were wider, and the 1300 models were of a different style. There were new badges front and rear, however, the rear lights remained unchanged on the estate. The styling of the original 1100 was done by the Italian company Pininfarina, who had also been responsible for the Austin A40, and hints of A40 styling, such as the short rear end, can be seen in these cars. The 1968 range of cars now consisted of two and four-door De Luxe saloons with 1100 engine, two or four-door Super De Luxe saloons with either 1100 or 1300 engines, and a Countryman estate with 1300 engine. The entry level model, now named De Luxe, had a different front dashboard to other models, with just a combined speedometer and fuel gauge like the original Mini. It also had fixed non-opening windows on the two-door model. Estate models had sliding rear side windows, and now came with a simulated wood finish side trim. An interesting point is that although the estate may appear, at a glance, to be longer than the saloon, it is

Above: 1300. Below: 1100.

actually the same length. A further model, the 1300 GT, was added to the range in late 1969. It was technically similar to the Riley 1300 which was discontinued, but differed in appearance as it featured a black vinyl roof, matt black radiator grille with red GT letters, and thick body side mouldings; it was only available as a four-door model.

Price in 1970: 1100 Super De Luxe £860, 1300 Super De Luxe £887, 1300 GT £996. Standard equipment on the Super De Luxe included water temperature gauge, full-width front parcel shelf and pockets in front doors, heater, windscreen washers, opening quarter lights in front doors and rear window on two-door models, and a single lever on steering column for indicators, headlight flasher, dipswitch and horn. Previously, the dipswitch had been on the floor and the horn was a button in the middle of the steering wheel. Optional equipment included radio, seatbelts, auxillary lights, reclining front seats, electrically heated rear window (saloon only), automatic transmission and more.

COLOURS: Early cars: Tartan red, Connaught green, Aquamarine, Alaskan blue, El Paso beige, Snowberry white, and Black. Later cars: Flame red, Connaught green, Bermuda blue, Blue Royale, Cumulus grey, Antelope, Fawn brown, Glacier white, and Black. Note: not all colours were available on all models. GT 1300 only: initially, Flame red, Glacier white, and Bronze yellow; later colours added to above included Blaze, Teal blue, and Limeflower.

ENGINE: Four-cylinder, OHV. 1100: bore 64.58mm, stroke 83.72mm, 1098cc (67.02in), maximum bhp 48 at 5100rpm, SU HS2 carburettor. 1300: bore 70.61mm, stroke 81.28mm, 1275cc (77.82in^3), maximum bhp 58 at 5250rpm, SU HS4 carburettor. 1300 GT as 1300 except maximum bhp 70 at 6000rpm, two SU HS2 carburettors.

GEARBOX: All four-speed, floor-mounted gear change, synchromesh on top three gears

Rear lights. Left: mark 1. Right: mark 2.

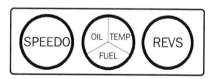

Above, 1300 GT instrument layout. Left, Super De Luxe. Note: rocker switches replaced the toggle type used on the mark 1 cars. Also note that the indicator switch is on the right-hand side of the steering column, as was usual before wiper controls were moved from the dashboard to the steering column.

(synchromesh on all gears from 1968), 1100
ratios: top 4.133, 3rd 5.83, 2nd 8.97, 1st
15.0, reverse 15.0. 1300 ratios: top 3.65, 3rd
5.16, 2nd 7.95, 1st 13.23, reverse 13.23.
1300 GT ratios: top 3.65, 3rd 5.23, 2nd 8.09,
1st 12.89, reverse 12.89. Final drive ratios:
1100 4.113:1, both 1300 models 3.65:1.
BRAKES: Lockheed with pressure limiting
valve, front 8-inch discs, rear 8-inch drums.
1300 GT had 8.4-inch front discs with option
of power assistance.
STEERING: Rack and pinion.
TYRES: 5.50 x 12, GT 145 x 12.
SUSPENSION: As 1100 mark 1.
DIMENSIONS: Length saloon and estate with
overriders, 12ft 2.75in (3.73m), GT and two-
door without overriders 12ft 1.81in (3.69m).
All other dimensions/weight as 1100 mark 1.
CAPACITIES: As 1100 mark 1.

*Above: An early estate without the side trim
applied to later cars (this car is actually a
Morris).*

Austin 1100/1300 mark 3

Front grilles: top left, 1100 mark 1; top right, 1100 mark 2; middle, 1300; bottom left, 1300 GT; bottom right, 1300 mark 3.

Left, Mini. Right, 1300, which has sufficient room for the battery. Also note the absence of radiator cowling on this later model.

Introduced in September 1971, and discontinued in June 1974, it was replaced by the Allegro that had been launched in May 1973. The Morris saloon was discontinued in 1971, replaced by the Marina, and the Morris Traveller estate and Wolseley 1300 were discontinued in 1973. The Vanden Plas 1300 was discontinued in June 1974. New front grilles, consisting of single or triple bright steel strips on a black mesh (similar to that used for the 1300 GT which had been released as a mark 2 model in 1969), replaced the more elaborate designs seen on the earlier 1100/1300 models, and front and rear badges were also changed. Another external change was the loss of overriders, and the indicator repeater flashers were removed from the front wings. Inside was a completely new style of dashboard with circular instruments, simulated wood-grain finish, and adjustable fresh air vents at the ends. There were new seats and carpets, the Super De Luxe also had a glove box, but gone were the door pockets. Hidden changes included altering the electrical system to negative earth, and replacing the dynamo with an alternator. All cars now had 8.4-inch front discs and gearbox ratios were revised.

Numbers produced: 389,000 mark 1, 398,000 mark 2, 221,500 mark 3, 52,000 1300 GT mark 1 and 2.

Prices in 1974: 1300 Super De Luxe £1175, 1300 GT £1362. Note: a Ford Escort 1300 XL was £1485.

Standard equipment for the De Luxe included a black instrument pod with speedometer and fuel gauge, combined key operated ignition/starter switch with steering column lock, heater, windscreen washers, and opening quarter lights in front doors. Super De Luxe had simulated wood-grain dashboard with speedometer, fuel and water temperature gauges, glove box on passenger side, armrests on all doors, carpet instead of rubber mat floor covering, and opening rear quarter lights on two-door model. GT, in addition to Super De Luxe, had a tachometer (revolution counter), black finish dashboard, reclining front seats, rear seat centre armrest and more.

COLOURS: Flame red, Blaze, Green mallard, Aqua, Teal blue, Midnight blue, Black, Glacier white, Bronze yellow, Harvest gold, and Limeflower.

Gear change diagram.

1973 specification

ENGINES: See mark 2 models.
GEARBOX: All four-speed, floor-mounted gear change, synchromesh on all gears, 1100 ratios: top 4.133, 3rd 5.91, 2nd 9.175, 1st 14.59, reverse 14.63. 1300 ratios: top 3.65, 3rd 5.22, 2nd 8.103, 1st 12.88, reverse 12.92. 1300 GT ratios: top 3.65, 3rd 4.93, 2nd 7.41, 1st 12.15, reverse 12.89. Front-wheel drive as 1100 mark 1, final drive ratio 1100 model 4.133:1, both 1300 models 3.65:1.
BRAKES: Lockheed, front 8.4-inch discs and rear 8-inch drums, power assistance now standard on 1300 GT.
STEERING: Rack and pinion.
TYRES: 5.50 x 12, GT 1300 145 x 12, spare wheel in a covered recess under the boot floor.
SUSPENSION: As 1100 mark 1.
DIMENSIONS: Length all models 12ft 1.81in (3.69m), all other dimensions as 1100 mark 1. Kerb weights: 1100 two-door 15cwt 2qtr 15lb (794kg), 1300 four-door 16cwt 1qtr 7lb (829kg), estate 16cwt 3qtr 7lb (853kg), all weights approximate.
CAPACITIES: As 1100 mark 1.

Austin 1800 mark 1

Introduced in 1964, a Morris model followed in 1966, and a Wolseley in 1967. Unlike the 1100/1300 range there were never any MG or Riley versions of the 1800, anyone desiring one of these marques had to choose between the front-wheel drive 1300 range or the rear-wheel drive Magnette and 4/72. This was the start of rationalisation of BMC models, and by 1970 there were no more Riley cars, and the final Wolseley model, the 18/22, was discontinued in 1975. The 1800 followed the transverse engine mounted, front-wheel drive formula of the 1100/1300 range, which became the standard format for all following Austin cars, with the exception of the 3-litre produced only from 1967 to 1971. Morris, however, not only continued producing rear-wheel drive cars, such as the Oxford and the Minor, up until 1971, but the Minor's replacement, the Marina, also had rear-wheel drive, and after 1975 it became the sole Morris model. Often referred to as the Landcrab, the 1800 was voted European Car of the Year in 1965, and successfully completed the London to Sydney rally in 1968, finishing in second place. Its strong bodyshell also made it popular with coachbuilders, who converted it into a hearse for funeral companies, and its doors were used on the Austin 3-Litre and Maxi.

It was the first Austin with a five-bearing crankshaft, the engine itself being derived from that used in the MGB. It also featured a handbrake fitted under the dashboard, although BMC had been fitting floor-mounted handbrakes for many years; the mark 3 models all had the floor-mounted type. Modifications and improvements occurred regularly during the first few years, so that by the time the Morris version appeared, most of the 'teething' problems associated with many new models were sorted. Problems included high oil consumption – sometimes caused by owners overfilling the cars after reinserting the dipstick the wrong way around – and also valve bounce when travelling at speed on motorways. This problem was cured by changing the final drive ratio from 4.178 to 3.88. Other changes made were the removal of the rear anti-roll bar, changing the

69

steering set up to reduce tyre scuffing, fitting different engine mounting rubbers and slight repositioning of the handbrake.

Number produced: 110,000 approximately.

Price when introduced: De Luxe saloon £809.

Standard equipment included water temperature gauge, headlight flasher, windscreen washer, heater with fresh air vents at either end of the full-width front parcel shelf, driver's sun visor, anti-glare interior mirror, front and rear door pockets, and side repeater indicators on front wings. De Luxe adds passenger sun visor, door scuff and tread plates, carpet instead of rubber mat floor covering, leather trimmed seats, opening rear quarter lights, overriders, and wheel trim discs. Optional extras included radio, reclining front seats, seatbelts and more.

COLOURS: Snowberry white, Maroon, Almond green, Persian blue, Cumulus grey, Canyon grey, Titian beige, and Black.

ENGINE: Four-cylinder, OHV, bore 80.26mm, stroke 88.9mm, 1798cc (109.75in³), maximum bhp 84 at 5300rpm, SU HS6 carburettor.

GEARBOX: Four-speed, floor-mounted gear change, all synchromesh gearbox, ratios: top 4.19, 3rd 5.80, 2nd 9.29, 1st 13.79, reverse 12.88. Later cars: top 3.88, 3rd 5.37, 2nd 7.99, 1st 12.78, reverse 11.94. Front-wheel drive with helical spur gears and open driveshafts with universal joints, final drive ratios: early cars, 4.19:1, later cars, 3.88:1.

BRAKES: Girling, power assisted with pressure limiting valve fitted to apportion more accurate braking between front and rear wheels. This should not to be confused with the more sophisticated anti-lock braking systems that started to appear on cars during the mid-

Instrument layout.

| TEMP | SPEEDO | FUEL |

Left (top and bottom): Morris 1800 mark 1. Right (top and bottom): Austin 1800 mark 1. Note the different front grille and rear lights.

eighties. Front 9.28-inch discs, rear 9-inch drums.

STEERING: Rack and pinion.

TYRES: 175 x 13.

SUSPENSION: Front independent with upper and lower arms and tie rods, swivel axles mounted on ball joints, rear independent with trailing arms, front and rear with interconnected Hydrolastic displacers.

DIMENSIONS: Length 13ft 8.19in (4.17m), width 5ft 6.75in (1.70m), height 4ft 8.25in (1.43m), wheel base 8ft 10in (2.69m), track front 4ft 8in (1.38m), rear 4ft 7.5in (1.36m), ground clearance 6.625in (16.83cm), turning circle 37ft 6in (11.3m), weight 1 ton 2cwt 2qtr 14lb (1150kg).

CAPACITIES: Fuel 10.5 gallons (47.7 litres). Boot 17.0ft³ (0.48m³).

Austin 1800 mark 2

Introduced in May 1968 to replace the mark 1 model, it had a new front grille, similar to that fitted to the Austin 1300. This grille was not as wide as that fitted to the mark 1, so larger front indicators were able to be fitted. Also new were revised rear lights, which were now vertical instead of horizontal and formed part of the rear wing, immediately differentiating it from the mark 1. The change from 13-inch to 14-inch wheels was probably less apparent. Seat surfaces were now vinyl not leather, but the dashboard had a simulated wood-grain finish, with the heater controls in the centre console, which also housed the ashtray and a recess for the optional radio. Two-speed wipers with electrically operated windscreen washers, new style door pockets without kick plates, flush fitting interior door handles, and modified window winder handles, together with a new lever on the steering column controlling headlight high/low beam, headlight flasher, horn, and indicators created a more modern looking interior. Under the bonnet, a revised cylinder head with bigger valves and an increased compression ratio raised power slightly; a more powerful model, the 1800S, which was equipped with two carburettors, was also available.

Number produced: 74,000 approximately, including 'S' models.

Prices in 1969: De Luxe saloon £1046, automatic £1146, 'S' £1105.

Standard equipment included water temperature gauge, headlight flasher, windscreen washer, heater with fresh air vents at either end of front parcel shelf, anti-glare interior mirror, front and rear door pockets, side repeater indicators on front wings, opening rear quarter lights, locking fuel flap, and overriders. Optional extras included radio, clock, reclining front seats, seatbelts, heated rear window, automatic transmission and more.

COLOURS: Glacier white, Damask red, Bermuda blue, Blue Royale, Midnight blue, Persian blue, Carlton grey, Racing green, Antelope, Bedouin, Limeflower, and Wild Moss.

ENGINE: Four-cylinder, OHV, bore 80.26mm, stroke 88.9mm, 1798cc (109.75in^3), maximum bhp 86.5 at 5400rpm, SU HS6 carburettor. S model maximum bhp 95.5 at 5700rpm, two SU HS6 carburettors.

GEARBOX: Four-speed, floor-mounted gear change, 3-speed automatic optional, all synchromesh gearbox, ratios: top 3.88, 3rd 5.35, 2nd 7.98, 1st 12.77, reverse 11.93. Front-wheel drive as 1800 mark 1, final drive ratio 3.88:1.

BRAKES: Girling, power assisted with pressure limiting valve, front 9.28-inch discs, rear 9-inch drums, S model front 9.7-inch discs, rear 9-inch drums.

STEERING: Rack and pinion, power assistance optional.

TYRES: 165 x 14.

SUSPENSION: As mark 1.

DIMENSIONS: Length 13ft 10.75in (4.24m), width 5ft 6.75in (1.70m), height 4ft 8.25in (1.43m), wheel base 8ft 10in (2.69m), track front 4ft 8in (1.38m), rear 4ft 7.5in (1.36m), ground clearance 6.625in (16.83cm), turning circle 37ft 6in (11.3m), weight 1 ton 2cwt 2qtr 14lb (1150kg).

CAPACITIES: Fuel 10.5 gallons (47.7 litres). Boot 17.0ft^3 (0.48m^3).

Left: Morris 1800 mark 2. Right: Austin 1800 mark 2.

Left: Austin and Morris 1800 mark 2 and 3 rear lights. Right: Wolseley 18/85.

Austin 1800 mark 3 and 2200

Introduced in March 1972, with a new model – the six-cylinder 2200 – replacing the 1800S, this entirely new engine which was subsequently carried over to the 18/22 and Princess, had been derived from the Austin Maxi four-cylinder engine; it was not just an 1800 engine with two extra cylinders. This new engine was called the 'E-series.' The six-cylinder A110 engine, the 'C-series,' was too long to be installed transversely, unlike the 'B-series' engine from the A60, which had been successfully turned around and fitted into the 1800. BMC had earlier been able to use the A-series engine from the Austin A35, mounting it transversely into the Mini. The experience gained when fitting the gearbox underneath the A-series enabled a similar arrangement to be adopted for the B-series when it was fitted into the 1800. Although Austin and Morris continued to produce the original four-cylinder 1800 alongside their new six-cylinder 2200 model,

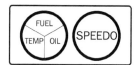

Left: 2200 instrument layout. Below: 1800.

TEMP | SPEEDO | FUEL

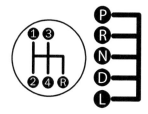

Left: Manual gear change diagram. Right: Optional automatic.

the Wolseley 18/85 four-cylinder models were discontinued, leaving only the Six. Both Austin models were discontinued in 1975 following the introduction of the 18/22. The extra length of the six-cylinder engine meant that the radiator could not be fitted against the inner wheelarch, as had been the case with other transversely mounted engines, so it had to be fitted at the front of the engine compartment in a more traditional manner. The advantage of this was that it kept water from being blown through the front grille, so a plastic cover was not needed to keep the electrical components dry. It did, however, mean that an electric fan had to be fitted, as it could no longer be driven by a belt at the front of the engine. The handbrake was moved from beneath the dashboard to a new location between the front seats, an alternator replaced the dynamo, and a larger fuel tank was fitted to the 2200. Visually, two new styles of front grille were fitted, enabling instant recognition of the two different models. At the rear of the car only badges with engine size identified the 1800 from the 2200, the overriders and S model style side trim were removed.

Numbers produced: 1800 mark 3 26,000, plus an unknown quantity of 2200 models.
Prices: 1800 £1412, 2200 £1448.
Standard equipment on the 1800 included water temperature gauge, heater, two-speed windscreen wipers, electric windscreen washers, combined ignition/starter with steering column lock, door bins of the original mark 1 style, and wood effect dashboard. The 2200 also had oil pressure gauge, glove box and more. Optional extras included radio, reclining front seats, automatic transmission, electrically heated rear window, power-assisted steering, and Rostyle wheels (2200 only). In 1974, hazard warning lights, an exterior door mirror, and heated rear window became standard equipment on both models.

COLOURS: Glacier white, Flame red, Midnight blue, Teal blue, Green Mallard, Harvest gold, Limeflower, and Wild Moss.
ENGINE: 1800, four-cylinder, OHV, bore 80.26mm, stroke 88.9mm, 1798cc (109.75in^3), maximum bhp 86.5 at 5400rpm,

Left: Morris 1800 mark 3. Right: Morris 2200. Note the different front grilles. Austin cars are identical with the exception of name badges.

SU HS6 carburettor. 2200, six-cylinder, OHC, bore 76.2mm, stroke 81.28mm, 2227cc (135.8in³), maximum bhp 110 at 5250rpm, two SU HS6 carburettors, later cars SU HIF6.
GEARBOX (both models): Four-speed, floor-mounted gear change, now rod rather than cable operated, 3-speed automatic optional, all synchromesh gearbox, ratios: top 3.88, 3rd 5.35, 2nd 7.99, 1st 12.77, reverse 11.91. Front-wheel drive as 1800 mark 1, final drive ratio 3.88:1.
BRAKES: Girling, power assisted with pressure limiting valve, front 9.28-inch discs, rear 9-inch drums, 2200 model front 9.7-inch discs, rear 9-inch drums.
STEERING: As mark 2.
TYRES: 165 x 14.
SUSPENSION: As mark 1.
DIMENSIONS: Length 13ft 10.75in (4.24m), width 5ft 6.75in (1.70m), height 4ft 8.25in (1.43m), wheel base 8ft 10in (2.69m), track front 4ft 8in (1.38m), rear 4ft 7.5in (1.36m), ground clearance 1800, 6.625in (16.83cm), 2200, 6.5in (16cm), turning circle 37ft 6in (11.3m), weight 1800, 1 ton 2cwt 3qtr (1155kg), 2200, 1 ton 3cwt 1qtr 13lb (1187kg).
CAPACITIES: Fuel 1800, 10.5 gallons (47.7 litres), 2200, 12.5 gallons (56.8 litres). Boot 17.0ft³ (0.48m³).
PRODUCTION TOTALS (for all 1800/2200 and 18/85 Six models: Austin – 221,000 (Sept 1964 to 1975); Morris – 105,000 (March 1966 to 1975); Wolseley – 61,000 (May 1967 to 1975).

Austin 3-Litre

Introduced in 1967, and discontinued in 1971, the 3-Litre was Austin's replacement for the A110 Westminster, which had been introduced as the A99 in 1959. However, unlike the A99/A110, there were never any Wolseley or Vanden Plas versions of the 3-Litre. In appearance, the 3-Litre resembled a large 1800, and did actually use the doors and central section from that model. It also had a ribbon type speedometer and Hydrolastic suspension, but there the similarities ended. The 1800 was a front-wheel drive car, whilst the 3-Litre had rear-wheel drive with the engine mounted in a traditional north to south, rather than transverse, position. This engine, which had a seven-bearing crankshaft, was a version of the BMC C-series engine, which had been used not only in the Westminster, but also the Austin Healey 3000 sports car.
Number produced: 9992.
Price when introduced: £1418.
Standard equipment included a clock, water temperature and oil pressure gauges,

ammeter, variable instrument lighting to prevent night time glare, headlight flasher, windscreen washer, heater with fresh air vents at either end of front dashboard, heater ducting to rear compartment, wood-trimmed dashboard and door trim tops, lockable glove box, ruched pockets in front doors and back of front seats, ashtrays in backs of front seats, armrests on front and rear doors, inner sides of front seats, and in the middle of the rear seat, opening

TEMP	SPEEDO	FUEL

Above: Instrument layout. Note: clock, ammeter, and oil pressure gauge were fitted in a separate unit in the centre of the dashboard.

front and rear quarter lights, side repeater indicators on front wings, reversing light, relay unit to dim rear indicators and brake lights when side lights are on, locking fuel flap, internal bonnet release, and overriders. Optional extras included radio, heated rear window, overdrive, and automatic transmission. Note: seatbelts were fitted at the dealership and incurred a fitting charge.

COLOURS: Glacier white, Damask red, Blue Royale, Persian blue, Blackberry, Carlton grey, and Limeflower.
ENGINE (1969): Six-cylinder, OHV, bore 83.3mm, stroke 88.9mm, 2912cc (177.8in^3), bhp 123.6 at 4500rpm, two SU HS6 carburettors.
GEARBOX: Four-speed, floor-mounted gear

change, overdrive or automatic optional, all synchromesh gearbox, ratios: o/d top 2.91, top 3.56, o/d 3rd 3.80, 3rd 4.65, 2nd 7.326, 1st 10.60, reverse 9.54. With automatic: top 3.56, 2nd 5.16, 1st 8.50, reverse 7.45.
REAR AXLE: Hypoid bevel, final drive ratio manual and automatic 3.56:1.
BRAKES: Girling, power assisted. Front 10.4-inch discs, rear 9-inch drums, handbrake floor-mounted between front seats.
STEERING: Power assisted, rack and pinion.
TYRES: 185 x 14.
SUSPENSION: Front with upper and lower wishbones, rear with semi-trailing arms, self-levelling with hydraulic rams operated by engine driven pump, front and rear with inter-connected Hydrolastic displacers.
DIMENSIONS: Length 15ft 5.69in (4.70m), width 5ft 6.75in (1.70m), height 4ft 8.75in (1.44m), wheel base 9ft 7.5in (2.93m), track front 4ft 8.25in (1.43m), rear 4ft 8in (1.42m), ground clearance 6.5in (16cm), turning circle 37ft 6in (11.43m), weight 1 ton 9cwt 1qtr 14lb (1492kg).
CAPACITIES: Fuel 14.5 gallons (66 litres). Boot 18.0ft³ (0.52m³).

Austin Maxi 1

Introduced in May 1969, the Austin Maxi introduced hatchback motoring to those that had perhaps previously purchased estate cars. There was never a Morris version of the Maxi; devotees of that marque had a choice of a four-door saloon or a two-door coupé version of the Marina, both introduced in 1971, with an estate following in 1972. All Marina's had rear-wheel drive. The Maxi, however, continued the growing trend of front-wheel drive, but unlike previous Austins it did not use any versions of the A-, B-, or

C-series engines that had been in service for many years. It had an entirely new engine, the E-series. This was an OHC unit with an all synchromesh five-speed gearbox, the fifth gear being overdrive. Early cars had the cable operated gear change which had been used in other BMC cars, and which felt less positive in action than the rod operated system that was subsequently introduced in 1970. Also introduced at this time was a 1748cc engine to supplement the original 1485cc engine. As with most cars, there were modifications made throughout its life. Generally these were to keep up with changing trends, such as the introduction of hazard warning lights, alternators, dual circuit brakes and heated rear

Above: Early dashboard and instrument layout.
Below: Later dashboard. Note the two stalks
on the steering column.

windows. A novel feature of the car was the ability to fold the rear seat backwards as well as forwards. The former position, when used in conjunction with the reclining front seats, provided a rudimentary bed. Not so new were the doors from the 1800 models, which were also being used on the Austin 3-Litre. An upmarket model, the HL, was introduced in 1972, and automatic transmission became available with the 1748cc engine in 1974. This was followed by an increase in the size of the petrol tank in 1975, and the replacement of the Hydrolastic suspension with Hydragas in 1978. Both the 1485cc and 1748cc engines were subsequently used in the Allegro.
Number produced: 486,273 (mark 1 and 2).
Price when introduced: 1500 £993, 1750 £1102, HL £1392.
Standard equipment in 1973 included water temperature gauge, heater with two-speed blower, two-speed wipers, windscreen washers (note no rear windscreen wiper/ washer), steering column stalk for headlight flasher, dipswitch, and indicators. Later cars also had a stalk for wipers/washer, combined ignition/starter and steering column lock, interior bonnet release, wood-trimmed dashboard, lockable glove box, full-width front parcel shelf, detachable rear parcel shelf, armrests on all side doors,

fully reclining front seats and folding rear seat, driver's door mirror, side repeater indicators on front wings, reversing light, and more. HL added simulated leather-bound steering wheel, padded vinyl dashboard instead of wood trim, dipping rear view mirror, vanity mirror on passenger sun visor, cigarette lighter, electrically operated windscreen washers, storage boxes on front doors, heated rear window, front bumper underriders, different front grille with HL badge, full-length chrome side moulding with coloured insert, and more. Optional extras included electrically heated rear window and cigarette lighter for 1500 and 1750 models (standard on HL), and automatic transmission with 1750 engines only. Note: a heated rear window became standard equipment for all models during 1974.

COLOURS 1970: Glacier white, Damask red, Flame red, Bermuda blue, Blue Royale, Teal blue, Blackberry, Connaught green, Porcelain green, Racing green, Bedouin, El Paso beige, Fawn beige, Limeflower, and Wild Moss.
COLOURS (1976): Glacier white, Tahiti blue, Damask red, Flamenco, Tundra, Citron, Bracken, Harvest gold.

1970 specification
ENGINE: Four-cylinder, OHC, bore 76.2mm, stroke 81.28mm, 1485cc (90.61in³), bhp 74

Top: Early Maxi. Bottom: Later 1500 Maxi mark 1.

Top: Maxi HL mark 1. Bottom: Maxi 1750 mark 1.

Above: Maxi mark 2.

at 5500rpm, compression ratio 9.0:1, SU HS6 carburettor.

GEARBOX: Five-speed, floor-mounted remote control gear change (early cars cable operated), all synchromesh, ratios: 5th 3.34, 4th 4.20, 3rd 5.76, 2nd 8.42, 1st 13.45, reverse 14.56. Front-wheel drive with open driveshafts and constant velocity joints, final drive ratio 4.2:1. Note: later 1500 had different ratios.

1973 specification

ENGINE: All four-cylinder, OHC, 1500 as 1970 specification, 1750, bore 76.2mm, stroke 95.75mm, 1748cc (106.63in³), bhp 84 at 5000rpm, compression ratio 8.75:1, SU HS6 carburettor, HL as 1750 except, 95 bhp at 5350rpm, compression ratio 9.5:1, two SU HS6 carburettors.

GEARBOX: Five-speed, floor-mounted remote control gear change, all synchromesh, 1500,

Gear change diagram.

ratios: 5th 3.131, 4th 3.938, 3rd 5.40, 2nd 7.892, 1st 12.609, reverse 13.653. 1750 models, ratios: 5th 3.169, 4th 3.647, 3rd 5.003, 2nd 7.309, 1st 11.678, reverse 12.644. Front-wheel drive with open driveshafts and constant velocity joints, final drive ratios 1500, 3.938:1, both 1750 models 3.647:1

BRAKES: Power assisted, front 9.68-inch discs, rear 8-inch drums, handbrake floor-mounted between the front seats.

STEERING: Rack and pinion.

TYRES: 1500 and 1750, 155 x 13, HL only 165 x 13.

SUSPENSION: Independent with interconnected Hydrolastic front and rear displacers.

DIMENSIONS/WEIGHT: Length 13ft 2.33in (4.022m), width 5ft 4.12in (1.629m), height 4ft 5.28in (1.403m), wheel base 8ft 8in (2.642m), track front 4ft 5.8in (1.367m), rear 4ft 5.2in (1.351m), ground clearance 5.5in (14cm), turning circle 33ft 9in (10.29m), weight 1500/1750 19cwt 2qtr 20lb (1000kg), HL 19cwt 3qtr 4lb (1005kg).

CAPACITIES: Fuel 9 gallons (40.9 litres), later cars 10.5 gallons (47.7 litres). Boot 12.6ft³ (0.36m³) or 50.9ft³ (1.45m³) with rear seat folded down.

Austin Maxi 2

Introduced in August 1980 and discontinued two years later in July 1982, the Maxi 2 was replaced by the Maestro, which was not actually released until 1983. The Maxi 2 range consisted of 1750 L, HL and HLS models and the 1500 was no longer available. The HLS model had appeared in 1979, taking over from the HL model, which remained in production but with a single carburettor and generally the same equipment as the 1500, including the wood-trimmed dashboard instead of the original padded dashboard. The Maxi 2 had new bumpers with black plastic end caps and inserts instead of the one piece bumpers of the Maxi 1. The front indicators and rear reversing lights were incorporated into the new bumpers and a single rear foglight was placed underneath the rear bumper. Smaller, revised shape side indicators were now placed further back on the front wings, behind the wheelarches instead of in front of them. There were general equipment upgrades over the mark 1 model with brochures proclaiming "loads better!" All models now came with a radio, front door bins and more. The windscreen

wiper and washer controls were now on a stalk on the steering column with a new delay wipe facility, but there was still no rear screen wiper/washer, something that other manufacturers who had started producing hatchback models were including as standard. Many of them, however, were still using four-speed gearboxes without the overdrive ratio that had been associated with the Maxi and its five-speed gearbox for over ten years.

Prices when introduced: L model £4630, HLS £4985. For comparison, the similarly sized Ford Escort GL with a 1600cc engine cost £4518, and a Vauxhall Astra L with only a 1300cc engine cost £4367

Standard equipment for the Maxi 2 L model included water temperature gauge, heater with two-speed blower, two-speed wipers with intermittent wipe facility, electric screen washers, radio, two sun visors with vanity mirror on passenger side and ticket pocket on driver's side. Twin stalks on steering column, with lights controlled by left hand side and wipers/washers on right, combined ignition starter and steering column lock, interior bonnet release, lockable glove box, full-width front parcel shelf, detachable rear parcel shelf, armrests on all side doors, fully reclining front seats and folding rear seat, driver's door mirror, side repeater indicators on front wings, hazard warning lights, rear foglight, reversing light, electrically heated rear window, and more. HL added walnut veneer dashboard, tinted glass, different seat trim and front grille, and larger tyres. HLS, in addition to HL features, had a matt finish burr walnut dashboard, and twin carburettors. Optional equipment included

Gear change diagram.

automatic transmission, and metallic paint finish.

ENGINE: Four-cylinder, OHC, bore 76.2mm, stroke 95.75mm, 1748cc (106.63in³), bhp 72 at 4900rpm, compression ratio 8.75:1, SU HS6 carburettor. HLS as above except bhp 91 at 5250rpm, compression ratio 9.5:1, two SU HS6 carburettors.

GEARBOX: Five-speed floor-mounted remote control gear change, all synchromesh, ratios: 5th 3.169, 4th 3.647, 3rd 5.003, 2nd 7.309, 1st 11.678, reverse 12.644. Front-wheel drive as Maxi 1, final drive ratio 3.647:1.

BRAKES: Dual circuit, power assisted, front 9.68-inch discs, rear 8-inch drums, handbrake floor-mounted between the front seats.

STEERING: Rack and pinion.

TYRES: L 155 x 13, HL and HLS 165 x 13.

SUSPENSION: As Maxi 1.

DIMENSIONS/WEIGHT: Length 13ft 3.7in (4.057m), width 5ft 4.12in (1.629m), height 4ft 7.6in (1.412m), wheel base 8ft 8in (2.642m), track front 4ft 5.8in (1.367m), rear 4ft 5.2in (1.351m), ground clearance 5.5in (14cm), turning circle 33ft 9in (10.29m), weight L 19cwt 1qtr 14lb (984kg), HL 19cwt 2qtr (990kg), HLS 19cwt 2qtr 10lb (995kg).

CAPACITIES: Fuel 10.5 gallons (47.7 litres). Boot as Maxi 1.

Austin Allegro 1

Introduced in May 1973 as a replacement for the 1100/1300 models, which continued in production for a short while, the Allegro was designed by Harris Mann, who was also responsible for the Triumph TR7 and later the Princess model, both sometimes referred to as the wedge shaped cars. The Allegro by contrast was considered more of a jelly mould shape, but apart from the mixed reviews about its styling, and the dislike of its quartic shaped steering wheel, the more serious issue was its build quality, earning it the nickname 'All-agro.' Poor build quality was a problem associated with many 1970s cars, at a time when factory strikes and stoppages were commonplace, some resulting in the so-called three-day week. Some of the Allegro's problems, however, were as a result of failure to follow correct procedures, with stories of bodies flexing when they were lifted incorrectly. The unpopular quartic steering wheel was replaced in 1975 by a conventional round one, and by this time the range had been revised, with some versions of the two-door model being axed, and an estate model added. Interestingly, the estate was simply referred to as the Allegro estate, not the Countryman, a name that had been previously applied to Austin estates since the 1950s. The original range at launch

consisted of the following models: 1100 and 1300 Deluxe, 1300 and 1500 Super Deluxe, 1500 Special, 1750 Sport and 1750 Sport Special. With the exception of the 1500 Special and 1750 Sport Special, all cars were available as two or four-door models. The 1750 Sport Special was renamed the 1750 HL in 1974, and gained an extra carburettor. The 1098cc and 1275cc engines were inherited from the Austin 1100 and 1300 models, but the 1485cc and 1748cc engines were derived from the E-series engine fitted in the Austin Maxi. The 1098cc and 1275cc engines had four-speed gearboxes, but the 1485cc and 1748cc engines were fitted with five-speed gearboxes, in which the fifth gear was effectively an overdrive. Three different styles of front grilles were used; the Deluxe models had simple vertical slats, the 1300

Super Deluxe had horizontal slats and all 1500 and 1750 models had a honeycomb arrangement.

Number produced 1973 to 1982:
1100 model 136,380; 1300 model 312,467 saloons, 37,202 estates; 1500 models 107,082 saloons, 20,172 estates; 1750 model 20,801 saloons. Allegro (1980 to 1982) 1.0-litre model 8246.

Prices when introduced: £973 to £1367. Standard equipment on the 1100 and 1300 Deluxe included a heater/fresh air ventilation system, water temperature gauge, two-speed wipers with flick wipe, electric windscreen washers, hazard warning lights, heated rear window, steering column lock, exterior door mirror, and more. The 1300 Super Deluxe adds armrests/door pulls, reclining front seats, fitted carpets, interior bonnet release, cigar lighter, and exterior metal trim and coachline. The 1500 Super Deluxe, in addition to the 1300 features, had twin horns, simulated wood facia, and special seat trim. The 1750 Sport in addition to Super Deluxe model features had a revolution counter, simulated wood insert on steering wheel and gearlever knob, sports style wheels, head restraints, and black panel on boot lid. The 1500 Special, in addition to the 1500

Super Deluxe features, had a clock, vanity mirror, dipping rear view mirror, lockable glove box, console, simulated wood effect on steering wheel and door trim, rear seat centre armrest, aluminium door tread strips, carpet and light in boot, special wheel trims, bright exterior sill moulding, vinyl roof, and reversing lights. The 1750 Sport Special, in addition to 1500 Special features had a revolution counter, simulated wood gearlever knob, head restraints and black panel on boot lid. Optional extras for the 1100 and 1300 models were power assisted brakes (standard on 1500 and 1750); on all models except 1100, automatic transmission; on 1500 models only, head restraints (standard on 1750); for all models, metallic paint finish.

Dashboard layouts. Left: 1100, 1300, 1500 models. Below: 1750 models.

COLOURS: Glacier white, Blaze, Bracken, Damask red, Aconite, Mirage, Tundra, Harvest gold, and metallics: Cosmic, Lagoon blue, Brazil, and Rheingold.

ENGINE: All Four-cylinder. 1100 models: OHV, bore 64.58mm, stroke 83.73mm, 1098cc (67in³), maximum bhp 48 at 5250rpm, SU HS4 carburettor. 1300 models: OHV, bore 70.61mm, stroke 81.28mm, 1275cc (78in³), maximum bhp 56 at 5400rpm, SU HS4 carburettor. 1500 models: OHC, bore 76.2mm, stroke 81.28mm, 1485cc (91in³), maximum bhp 68 at 5500rpm, SU HS6 carburettor. 1750 models: OHC, bore 76.2mm, stroke 95.76mm, 1748cc (107in³), maximum bhp 91 at 5250rpm, two SU HS6 carburettors (from 1974 – earlier cars had a single SU carburettor).

GEARBOX: Four-speed, floor-mounted gear change, all synchromesh gearbox. 1100 ratios: top 4.13, 3rd 5.91, 2nd 9.17, 1st 14.58, reverse 14.62. 1300 ratios: top 3.94, 3rd 5.63, 2nd 8.75, 1st 13.91, reverse 13.95. 1500 and 1750 models were five-speed, all synchromesh, ratios: top 3.169, 4th 3.647, 3rd 5.00, 2nd 7.308, 1st 11.656, reverse 12.644. Front-wheel drive, open shafts with constant velocity joints, final drive ratio 1100 model 4.13:1, 1300 model 3.94:1, 1500 and 1750 models 3.647:1. Note: both 1100 and 1300 models used the same gearbox internal components but with different final drive ratios.

BRAKES: Front 9.68-inch discs, rear 8-inch drums, power assisted with 1500 and 1750 models.

STEERING: Rack and pinion.

TYRES: 1100, 1300, 1500 models, 145 x 13, 1750 models, 155 x 13.

SUSPENSION: Front unequal length suspension arms, trailing tie rods, rear trailing arms with interconnected front and rear Hydragas displacer units.

DIMENSIONS: Length saloon 12ft 7.67in (3.85m), length estate 12ft 11.22in (3.943m), width 5ft 3.52in (1.61m), height 4ft 7.04in (1.398m), wheel base 8ft 0.14in (2.44m), track front 4ft 5.62in (1.362m), rear 4ft 5.7in (1.364m), ground clearance 6.3in (16cm), turning circle 33ft 2.4in (10.1m), weight, four-door cars: 1100/1300 Deluxe 16cwt 1qtr 27lb (838kg), 1300 Super Deluxe 16cwt 3qtr 25lb

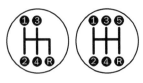

Gear change diagrams. Left: four-speed. Right: five-speed.

Allegro mark 1 front grilles. Above left: Deluxe. Above right: Super Deluxe. Left: Sport/Sport Special.

Top: Saloon. Bottom: estate, which had a flat rear panel, better suited for relocating the rear number plate when a tow bar was fitted.

(862kg), 1500 Super Deluxe 17cwt 2qtr 0lb (889kg), 1500 Special and all 1750 models 17cwt 3qtr 23lb (912kg). Two-door cars: 1100/1300 Deluxe 16cwt 0qtr 23lb (823kg), 1300 Super Deluxe 16cwt 2qtr 4lb (840kg), 1500 Super Deluxe 17cwt 0qtr 16lb (871kg), 1750 Sport 17cwt 1qtr 14lb (883kg).
CAPACITIES: Fuel 10.5 gallons (47.7 litres). Boot saloon 15ft³ (0.42m³).

Austin Allegro 2

Introduced in October 1975, the Allegro range was reduced from twelve saloon models to seven: 1100 Deluxe, 1300 Super, 1500 Super, 1500 Special, 1750 HL, with only the 1100 and 1300 being available as both two- and four-door models. There were also two estate models available, the 1300 and 1500 Super. All models now featured the honeycomb front grille previously reserved for the 1500 and 1750 models, and there were general equipment upgrades, with the 1100 models receiving much of the equipment previously reserved for the 1300 models. The rear seat was moved back five inches to improve rear legroom. Other improvements introduced during the production life of the Allegro 2 included dual circuit brakes and the fitting of power assisted brakes to all models, not just the 1500 and 1750 models.

Numbers produced: See Allegro mark 1
Price when introduced: £1541 to £2180. Note: a 1750 HL Maxi cost £2320. Standard equipment on the 1100 Deluxe included heater/fresh air ventilation system with two-speed fan, water temperature gauge, two-speed wipers with flick wipe and electric windscreen washers controlled by

a single lever on the side of the steering column, hazard warning lights, front parcel shelf, steering column lock, interior bonnet release, armrests/door pulls, fitted carpets, plastic sill guards, exterior door mirror, heated rear window, inertia reel front seatbelts and anchorages for rear seatbelts, and more. The 1300 Super adds lockable glove box, cigar lighter, reclining front seats, dipping interior mirror, rear seat centre armrest, reversing lights, bright door cappings, and double coachline. The 1500 Super, in addition to 1300 Super features, had twin horns, triple coachline, and five-speed gearbox. The 1500 Special, in addition to 1500 Super features, had a clock, two foglights, and boot light. The 1750 HL, in addition to the 1500 Special features, had a revolution counter, two black exterior mirrors, and lockable fuel filler cap. Optional extra on all models was metallic paint finish, on all 1300/1500 models automatic transmission, and 1100/1300 models only, power assisted brakes.

COLOURS (1976): 1100/1300 models: Tahiti blue, Glacier white, Damask red, Flamenco, Sand Glow, and Antique Gold. 1500/1750 models: Glacier white, Damask red, Flamenco, Sand Glow, Antique gold, and metallics, Astral blue, Brazil, and Reynard.
ENGINE/GEARBOX:
As Allegro mark 1.

Above: Instrument layout. Later Super models had a clock in the dashboard, and HL models had a revolution counter. Note: Early Super models and all HL models had a clock in the centre console.

Gear change diagrams. Left: Four-speed. Right: Five-speed.

BRAKES/STEERING/TYRES/SUSPENSION:
As Allegro mark 1.
DIMENSIONS: Length saloon 12ft 7.67in
(3.85m), length estate 12ft 11.22in (3.943m),
width 5ft 3.52in (1.61m), height 4ft 7.04in
(1.398m), wheel base 8ft 0.14in (2.44m),
track front 4ft 5.62in (1.362m), rear 4ft
5.7in (1.364m), ground clearance 6.3in
(16cm), turning circle 33ft 2.4in (10.1m),
weight, four-door cars: 1100 Deluxe 16cwt
2qtr 1lb (839.3kg), 1300 Super 16cwt
2qtr 27lb (851kg), 1500 Super 17cwt 1qtr
21lb (886kg), 1500 Special 17cwt 2qtr 0lb
(889kg), 1750HL 17cwt 2qtr 16lb (896kg).
Two-door cars: 1100 Deluxe 16cwt 1qtr
8lb (829kg), 1300 Super 16cwt 2qtr 3lb
(839.6kg), estates: 1300 Super 17cwt 2qtr
8lb (892.7kg), 1500 Super 18cwt 1qtr 8lb
(930.8kg).
CAPACITIES: Fuel 10.5 gallons (47.7 litres).
Boot saloon 9.05ft³ (0.26m³), estate 10.25ft³
(0.29m³), with seat down 53.06ft³ (1.50m³).

Austin Allegro 3

Introduced in September 1979, the Allegro
3 now featured a new engine – a 1.0-litre
unit that would also appear in the Metro,
launched a few months later in 1980; the
1098cc engine was gone. Also new was
a revised front grille, now with a Leyland
badge, side indicators and large black

plastic front and rear bumpers, as also
found on the Morris Ital. However, the Austin
Metro and Ambassador had smaller black
bumpers. Some Allegro models also had
four round headlights, but by 1982 this
feature had disappeared with all models
having the original rectangular ones. The
1982 saloon range comprised of the 1.0L,
1.3L, 1.3HL, 1.5HL, 1.7HL auto, and the
estate models were the 1.3L, 1.3HL, 1.5HL,
1.7HL auto. Power assisted, dual circuit
brakes with front discs were now standard
equipment on every model, and revised
rear lights incorporated the reversing lights,
while the rear foglights were fitted below
the bumper. The Allegro 3 was discontinued
in March 1982, it and the Austin Maxi both
replaced by the Austin Maestro, which was
not introduced until March 1983.

Numbers produced: See Allegro mark 1.
Prices when introduced: 1300L £4059,
1500L estate £4512, 1750HL £4900. For
comparison purposes a Metro 1.3 S cost
£3995.

Standard equipment for 1981 L models
included a heater/fresh air ventilation
system with two-speed fan, water
temperature gauge, two-speed wipers with
flick wipe and electric windscreen washers,
hazard warning lights, steering column
lock, armrests/door pulls, fitted carpets,
dipping interior mirror, exterior door mirror,
sill guards, heated rear window, inertia reel
seatbelts, side repeater indicators, single
coachline, and more. HL adds a clock, cigar
lighter, radio, reclining front seats, rear seat
centre folding arm rest, double coachline,
and locking fuel filler cap. HLS, in addition to
HL features, had a tachometer, cigar lighter,
centre floor-mounted console, intermittent
wipe facility for windscreen wipers, glove
box light, tinted glass, front seat headrests,
seats and door panels with velour trim,
bright sill tread steps, bright inserts in
bumpers, silver and black side rubbing
strips, two black exterior mirrors, four
circular headlights, and front foglights. All
estate models had a rear window wiper and

washer, and two exterior mirrors in addition
to the equipment already listed. Only HL
models had a carpeted load compartment
area.

*Gear change diagrams. Left :
Four-speed. Middle: Five-speed.
Right: Automatic.*

*Rear light
arrangements.
Top: Allegro 1
and 2. Bottom:
Allegro 3. Note
the different
lights, bumpers,
and position
of rear number
plates.*

COLOURS (1980): Ermine white, Vermilion red, Pageant blue, Black, Applejack, Russet brown, Champagne, and Snapdragon. The metallics were Denim blue, Tara green, and Oyster.
ENGINE: All four-cylinder. 1.0 models: OHV, bore 64.58mm, stroke 76.32mm, 998cc (61in^3), maximum bhp 44 at 5250rpm, SU HIF38 carburettor. 1.3 models: OHV, bore 70.62mm, stroke 81.28mm, 1275cc (78in^3), maximum bhp 62.7 at 5600rpm, SU HIF44 carburettor. 1.5 models, OHC, bore 76.2mm, stroke 81.28mm, 1485cc (91in^3), maximum bhp 77 at 5750rpm, two SU HIF4 carburettors. 1.7 HL model: OHC, bore 76.2mm, stroke 95.76mm, 1748cc (107in^3), maximum bhp 72 at 4900rpm, SU HIF6 carburettor. 1.7 HLS as 1.7 HL except: maximum bhp 90 at 5500rpm, two SU HIF6 carburettors. Note: 1.7 HLS with automatic transmission as 1.7 HL.
GEARBOX: Four-speed, floor-mounted gear change, all synchromesh gearbox. 1.0 ratios: top 4.33, 3rd 6.17, 2nd 9.47, 1st 15.80, reverse 15.89. 1.3 ratios: top 3.765, 3rd 5.365, 2nd 8.23, 1st 13.73, reverse 13.81. 1.5 and 1.7: five-speed, all synchromesh, ratios: top 3.169, 4th 3.647, 3rd 5.00, 2nd 7.308, 1st 11.656, reverse 12.644. 1.7 with four-speed automatic, ratios: top 3.8, 3rd 5.49, 2nd 6.866, 1st 9.926, reverse 9.926. Front-wheel drive, as Allegro mark 1, final drive ratios: 1.0 model 4.33:1, 1.3 model 3.765:1, 1.5 and 1.7 models 3.647:1, 1.7 automatic 3.8:1. Note: 1.0 and 1.3 models used the same gearbox internal parts but with different final drive ratios.
BRAKES: Power assisted, dual circuit, front 9.68-inch discs, rear 8-inch drums.
STEERING: Rack and pinion.
TYRES: L 145 x 13, all other models 155 x 13.
SUSPENSION: As Allegro mark 1.
DIMENSIONS: Length saloon 12ft 9.85in (3.91m), length estate 13ft 1.2in (3.993m), width 5ft 3.52in (1.61m), height saloon 4ft 6.84in (1.393m), estate 4ft 8.03in (1.422m) wheel base 8ft 0.14in (2.44m), track front 4ft 5.62in (1.362m), rear 4ft 5.7in (1.364m), ground clearance 6.3in (16cm), turning circle 33ft 2.4in (10.1m), weights, four-door cars: L 16cwt 1qtr 18lb (834kg), 1.3 L 16cwt 2qtr 9lb (843kg), 1.3 HL 17cwt 0qtr 14lb (870kg), 1.5 HL 17cwt 2qtr 20lb (899kg), 1.3 HLS 17cwt 1qtr 4lb (879kg), 1.5 and 1.7 HLS 17cwt 3qtr 10lb (907kg). Two-door cars: L 16cwt 0qtr 2lb (814kg), 1.3 HL 16cwt 2qtr 19lb (848kg), estates 1.3 L 16cwt 3qtr 0lb (851kg), 1.3 HL 17cwt 2qtr 24lb (900kg), 1.5 HL 18cwt 1qtr 2lb (928kg). Note: weights above are for manual cars, automatics are generally 46lb (21kg) heavier. 1.7 HL estate automatic 18cwt 2qtr 26lb (939kg).
CAPACITIES: As Allegro mark 2.

Austin and Princess 1800, 1800 HL, 2200 HL

Above, a Princess 2200HL. Below, an 1800.

Introduced in March 1975 and advertised as "The car that's got it all together," this model replaced the 1800 mark 3 and 2200, and it was an entirely new design by Harris Mann. Initially, there were Austin, Morris and Wolseley variants of the car, with the Wolseley model having its own unique frontal treatment, a full vinyl roof, and special wheel trims. It was also better equipped internally. The Hydrolastic suspension used in earlier front-wheel drive Austins was replaced by Hydragas suspension – another idea developed by Alex Moulton, which had originally been introduced with the Austin Allegro. To describe it in its simplest form, this new system used pressurised nitrogen units instead of rubber cones within the interconnected front and rear suspension. With the proliferation of cars now wearing Austin, Morris and Wolseley badges – there were 1800, 1800HL and 2200HL Austin and Morris models – the decision was made to simplify the range, and the car was renamed Princess, with four models – the 1800, 1800HL, 2200 HL and 2200 HLS – instead of the original seven, with

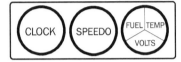

Above: instrument layout for HL and HLS models.

the new HLS model replacing the Wolseley. Thus, by September 1975, there were no more Wolseley cars, and the sole remaining Morris model was the Marina. The 1800 used a 1798cc version of the B-series engine (which had first been used in the MGB introduced in 1962, and subsequently used in the front-wheel drive Austin and Morris 1800 of 1964), whilst the 2200 used

Gear change diagram.

transmission, head restraints, metallic paint finish, and, for HL models only, a full vinyl covered roof. Standard equipment for the Princess range, in addition to the above: 1800 HL model, twin circular tungsten headlights, 2200 HLS, velour trimmed seats, height adjustable passenger seat, ruched door pockets, carpet in boot, tinted glass, vinyl covered roof, plastic inserts in bumpers, and more.

COLOURS (1975 18/22 model):
Glacier white, Damask red, Flamenco, Tahiti blue, Harvest gold, Citron, and metallics: Lagoon blue, Cosmic blue, Brazil, Rhine gold.
COLOURS (1976 Princess model): As 1975 colours except Reynard metallic replaced Rhine gold.
ENGINE: 1800 models: four-cylinder, OHV, bore 80.26mm, stroke 89.0mm, capacity 1798cc (109.7in³), maximum bhp 82 at 5200rpm, SU HS6 carburettor. 2200 models: six-cylinder, OHC, bore 76.2mm, stroke 81.28mm, 2227cc (135.8in³), maximum bhp 110 at 5250rpm, two SU HIF6 carburettors.
GEARBOX: All models, four-speed, floor-mounted gear change, three-speed automatic optional, all synchromesh gearbox, ratios: top 3.72, 3rd 5.13, 2nd 7.66, 1st 12.24, reverse 11.42. Front-wheel drive, open shafts with constant velocity joints, final drive ratio 3.72:1.
BRAKES: Power assisted, dual circuit, front 10.6-inch discs, rear 9-inch drums, handbrake between front seats.
STEERING: Rack and pinion, power assisted on 2200 models.
TYRES: 185 x 14.
SUSPENSION: Front wishbone style upper and lower transverse arms, rear trailing arms with interconnected front and rear Hydragas units.
DIMENSIONS: Length 14ft 7.5in (4.455m), width 5ft 8in (1.727m), height 4ft 7.5in (1.409m), wheelbase 8ft 9.25in (2.673m), track front 4ft 10in (1.473m), rear 4ft 9.5in (1.457m), ground clearance 6.45in (16.4cm), turning circle 37ft 10in (11.53m), kerb weight 1800 and 1800 HL, 1 ton 2cwt 3qtr 9lb (1160kg), 2200 HL, 1 ton 3cwt 2qtr 6lb (1197kg), 2200 HLS, 1 ton 3cwt 3qtr 17lb (1215kg).
CAPACITIES: Fuel tank 16 gallons (72.7 litres). Boot 18.8ft³ (0.532m³).

a six-cylinder version of the E-series engine that had been used in four-cylinder form in the Austin Maxi.
Number produced (1975 to 1982): 1800 models 84,867, 2200 models 63,443, 1700 models 41,134, 2000 models 35,498.
Price in 1975: Austin 1800 £2237, 2200 HL £2665.
Standard equipment for the Austin 1800 models were water temperature gauge, heater with three-speed fan, parcel shelves front and rear, lockable glove box, reclining front seats, height adjustable driver's seat, armrests on all doors, dipping rear view mirror, heated rear window, two-speed wipers with flick-wipe and electric windscreen washers controlled by a single lever on the side of the steering column, combined ignition switch and steering column lock, interior bonnet release, two exterior door mirrors, reversing lights, hazard warning lights, and inertia reel front seatbelts. HL model added a battery indication meter, clock, rear seat folding armrest, door sill tread plates, vanity mirror on passenger sun visor, floor console surrounding gearlever, lockable fuel cap, coachline, wheel trim rings, vinyl-covered rear quarter panels and bright door frame and wheelarch mouldings. On the 2200 model only there was power assisted steering. Optional extras included automatic

Princess 2, 1700 L, 1700 HL, 2000 HL, 2200 HL, 2200HLS

Introduced in 1978 to replace the Princess mark 1, the Princess 2 featured two new engines: the new 'O-series' in 1700cc and 2000cc form. The 1800 model, powered by the B-series engine was now gone. (The B-series had been a stalwart of the BMC range since 1954, having grown from 1489cc to 1622cc in 1961, and then to 1798cc for use in the MGB in 1962, followed by being mounted transversally in the Austin and Morris 'Landcrab' models of 1964). Initially, both 1700 models and the 2000 model featured twin circular tungsten headlights, with only the 2200 HLS retaining the original trapezoidal halogen headlights and full vinyl roof covering. However, this changed in 1979 when two new models were added to the range: the 1700 HLS and 2000 HLS. At this time equipment was no longer dependent on engine size. All L and HL models had four headlights, and all HLS models had the trapezoidal headlights and vinyl roof covering. The only way to identify each exact model was by reference to the badge on the boot lid. The 2200 HLS was, however, the only model to have power assisted steering as standard; it was available as an option on all the other models.

Price when introduced: 1700L £3781, 1700HL £4068, 2000HL £4254, 2200 HL £4599, 2200 HLS £5123.
Standard equipment (1978) on Austin 1700 L models included a fuel gauge, water temperature gauge, heater with three-speed fan, parcel shelves front and rear, lockable glove box, reclining front seats, height adjustable driver's seat, armrests on all doors, dipping rear view mirror, heated rear window, two-speed wipers with flick-wipe and electric windscreen washers controlled by a single lever on the side of the steering column, combined ignition switch and steering column lock, interior bonnet release, twin exterior door mirrors, reversing lights, hazard warning lights, and inertia reel front seatbelts. HL model adds a battery indication meter, clock, wood finish facia, rear seat folding armrest, door sill

On this page, KPV 200V is a 1700HL, and EJO 141V is a 2000 HLS.

tread plates, vanity mirror on passenger sun visor, floor console surrounding gearlever, lockable fuel cap, coachline, wheel trim rings, vinyl-covered rear quarter panels and bright door frame and wheelarch mouldings.

Left: Princess 1. Right: Princess 2. Note the different style of front grille and rear badges.

Instrument layout for HL models.

HLS model adds radio, velour trimmed seats, height adjustable passenger seat, head restraints, ruched door pockets, tinted glass, rear passenger reading lights, vinyl covered roof, plastic inserts in bumpers, carpet in boot, and more. Optional extras included automatic transmission, power assisted steering (standard on 2200), head restraints, and metallic paint finish. For HL models only a full vinyl covered roof. For 1979 all models had a clock, centre console, radio and rear foglight fitted as standard equipment.

COLOURS: Ermine white, Carmine, Vermilion red, Pageant blue, Russet brown, Champagne, Sand Glow, and Snapdragon. Metallics in Denim blue, Tara green, Reynard, and Oyster.
ENGINE: 1700 models: four-cylinder, OHC, bore 85mm, stroke 76mm, capacity 1700cc

On this page UHA 851X is a 1.7 HL, and UJK 424T is a 1700 HL.

Gear change diagram.

(103.7in³), maximum bhp 87 at 5200rpm, SU HIF6 carburettor. 2000 models: four-cylinder, OHC, bore 85mm, stroke 89mm, capacity 1994cc (121.6in³), maximum bhp 93 at 4900rpm, SU HIF6 carburettor. 2200 models: six-cylinder, OHC, bore 76.2mm, stroke 81.28mm, 2227cc (135.8in³), maximum bhp 110 at 5250rpm, two SU HIF6 carburettors.

GEARBOX: All models, four-speed, floor-mounted gear change, all synchromesh gearbox, ratios: top 3.72, 3rd 5.13, 2nd 7.66, 1st 12.24, reverse 11.42. Front-wheel drive, as Princess mark 1, final drive ratio 3.72:1. With optional three-speed automatic, ratios: top 3.83, 2nd 5.55, 1st 9.12, reverse 8.00, final drive ratio 3.83:1.

BRAKES/STEERING/TYRES/SUSPENSION: As Princess mark 1.

DIMENSIONS: Length 14ft 7.5in (4.455m), width 5ft 8in (1.727m), height 4ft 7.5in (1.409m), wheelbase 8ft 9.25in (2.673m), track front 4ft 10in (1.473m), rear 4ft 9.5in (1.457m), ground clearance 6.45in (16.4cm), turning circle 37ft 10in (11.53m), kerb weight 1700 L, 1 ton 2cwt 1qtr 23lb (1141kg), 1700 and 2200 HL, 1 ton 2cwt 2qtr 3lb (1145kg), 1700 and 2000 HLS, 1 ton 2cwt 2qtr 23lb (1154kg), 2200 HLS, 1 ton 3cwt 3qtr 17lb (1215kg).

CAPACITIES: As Princess mark 1.

Austin Ambassador

Introduced in March 1982 to replace the Princess, this was the hatchback that many thought the Princess should have been. The doors were carried over from the Princess, but the other bodywork, although retaining the wedge shape of the Princess, was new. Offered with 1.7 or 2.0 four-cylinder engines, the six-cylinder 2.2-litre engine was no longer available. The four-speed gearbox, however, remained, even though other Austin cars had been available with a five-speed gearbox for a number of years.

The model range now consisted of 1.7 L, 1.7 HL, 2.0 HL, 2.0 HLS, and a Vanden Plas 2.0. The Vanden Plas name had also been applied to a version of the Allegro, but unlike the Allegro the Vanden Plas Ambassador did not have its own distinctive grille, just an additional piece of trim on the bonnet. The Champagne-coloured car in this section is a Vanden Plas model and has bright inserts in the bumper and side trim. This feature was later added to other models. Note also, it has a standard fitted sunroof, a metal item, not the glass sun roofs that were beginning to appear on Ford and Vauxhall cars during the 1980s.

Number produced: 43,500.

Price when introduced: 1.7 HL £5335, 1.7 HL £5995, 2.0 HL £6299, 2.0 HLS £6998. Standard equipment on the L model included a water temperature gauge and a large range of warning lights, radio, heater/fresh air ventilation system with three-speed fan, lockable glove box, front floor console with ashtray, driver's sun visor with pocket, passenger sun visor with vanity mirror, front courtesy light, fully reclining front seats, folding bench type rear seat, drivers door mirror, two-speed wipers with flick wipe, heated rear window, and lockable fuel filler flap. HL model adds height adjustable driver's seat, front seat headrests, rear seat centre armrest, front door bins, rear courtesy light, glove box light, black sill mouldings and black side trim. HLS, in addition to HL features, had a clock, econometer (a vacuum gauge), variable instrument lighting, radio/stereo

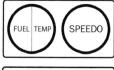

Instrument layouts. Top: For the L and HL models. Bottom: For the HLS models.

cassette player with four speakers, internal adjustment for door mirror, locking the driver's door automatically locked all the other doors (not the remote push button type central locking associated with more modern cars), rear window wash/wipe, tinted glass, electrically operated front windows, power steering, and two carburettors with the 2.0-litre engine. Vanden Plas model added map pockets on back of front seats, rear seat headrests, velour trimmed seats, carpeted lower halves of the doors, both door mirrors adjustable from inside, steel sliding sunroof, front foglights, and bright inserts in bumpers and side trim. Optional extras for the 1.7 L were passenger door mirror, internal adjustment of exterior

mirrors, rear seatbelts, radio/cassette unit, rear speakers, clock, front headrests, power assisted steering and automatic transmission. In addition, HL model options were tinted windows and sunroof. For 1983 there were upgrades for the HL model: instead of the single carburettor 2.0-litre engine, it now had the 2.0-litre unit with two carburettors previously used in the HLS and Vanden Plas models, a radio/cassette, rear wash wipe, bright bumper and side trim inserts, and more.

COLOURS (1982): Ermine white, Champagne, Emberglow, Nautilus blue, and Black. Metallics were Silver leaf, Cashmere gold, Oporto red, and Opaline green.

COLOURS (1983): Arum white, Ratan beige, Monza red, Clove brown, Eclipse blue, and Black. Metallics were Silver leaf, Cashmere gold, Oporto red, Opaline green, and Zircon blue.

ENGINE: Four-cylinder, OHC. 1.7 models: bore 85mm, stroke 76mm, capacity 1700cc (103.7in^3), maximum bhp 83 at 5200rpm, SU HIF6 carburettor. 2.0 HL: bore 85mm, stroke 89mm, capacity 1994cc (121.6in^3), maximum bhp 92 at 4900rpm, SU HIF6 carburettor, later cars with two SU carburettors. 2.0 HLS as 2.0 HL but with maximum bhp 100 at 5250rpm, two SU HIF6 carburettors.

GEARBOX: All models, four-speed, floor-mounted gear change, all synchromesh gearbox, ratios: top 3.72, 3rd 5.35, 2nd 8.25, 1st 13.19, reverse 11.65. Front-wheel drive, open shafts with constant velocity joints, final drive ratio 3.72:1. With optional three speed automatic, ratios: top 3.83, 2nd 5.55, 1st 9.12, reverse 8.00, final drive ratio 3.83:1.

BRAKES: Power assisted, dual circuit, front 10.6-inch discs, rear 90-inch drums, handbrake between front seats.

STEERING: Rack and pinion, power assisted on 2.0 HLS, optional on others.

TYRES: 185 x 14.

SUSPENSION: Front double wishbone style arms, rear trailing arms with interconnected front and rear Hydragas units.

DIMENSIONS: Length 14ft 11.3in (4.55m), width 5ft 8.1in (1.70m), height 4ft 7.25in (1.40m), wheelbase 8ft 9.25in (2.67m), track front 4ft 10.2in (1.48m), rear 4ft 9.54in (1.45m), ground clearance 6.7in (17.1cm), turning circle 37ft 10in (11.53m), kerb weight varies according to model but typically 1 ton 4cwt 3qtr 12lb (1263kg).

CAPACITIES: Fuel tank 16 gallons (72.7 litres). Boot 17.1ft^3 (0.48m^3) or 54.7ft^3 (1.55m^3) with rear seat folded down.

Gear change diagram.

Austin Metro

Introduced in October 1980 and re-badged as a Rover 100 in 1995, the Metro was discontinued in 1997. There were also MG and Vanden Plas versions of the Metro, but both of these had much shorter lives. Often referred to as the Austin Mini Metro it was never going to be able to directly replace the much loved Mini, but its introduction did see the end of the Mini Clubman model. Initially available only as a three-door hatchback, although some of its competitors such as the Volkswagen Polo and Vauxhall Chevette were also available as a saloon, a five-door version of the Metro appeared in 1984, a variant not offered by Vauxhall or Volkswagen. Models at launch were Standard 1.0, 1.0 L, 1.0 HLE, 1.3 S, 1.3 HLS, with names such as City and Mayfair subsequently being used to replace basic and HLE models. Basic models had been aimed at the fleet market, for example driving schools, and there were also a number of special editions introduced at various times; These included the Moritz, Advantage, Red Hot, and Jet Black. In 1984, the front end received a styling change, and there were equipment upgrades. In 1987 further changes were made to improve the car, including measures to quieten the interior noise. Also at this

point, the Austin badges disappeared, and like the Maestro and Montego, only a bonnet badge, like the Rover 'long-ship' badge, and model designation badges on the rear became the norm. For 1990, there were new front and rear bumpers, restyled front wings, headlights, bonnet, and rear lights. In 1990, the Rover name appeared on the back of the Metro, together with 111 or 114 badges, and a Rover badge like that on the Rover 200, 400 and 600 models was fitted to the bonnet. Other changes made during it's life included moving the fuel filler flap on three-door models, following raised concerns about petrol spillage whilst cornering.

Number produced: 2,078,218

Prices when introduced: Standard Metro list price: £2484 plus car tax (£207) and VAT (£403.65), giving a total of £3094.65, 1.3 HLS list price: £3448 plus car tax (£287.33) and VAT (£560.30) giving a total of £4295.63. An optional glass or steel sunroof was £111 inclusive of car tax and VAT. The SUPERCOVER scheme, which enabled the standard one year warranty to be extended to two years, cost from £45 to £115 dependent on engine size and whether or not AA breakdown service was included. Equipment at launch for the Standard model included water temperature gauge, trip mileage recorder, heater and fresh

air vents with two-speed fan, two-speed wipers with flick wipe, front windscreen washers, driver's sun visor with ticket pocket, passenger sun visor, front parcel shelf, removable rear parcel shelf, folding rear seat, dipping interior mirror, driver's door mirror, heated rear window, inertia reel seatbelts, front side lights and indicators mounted in bumper, side repeater indicator lights, rear foglight, hazard warning lights, rear mudflaps, and more. The Metro L also came with rear screen wash/wipe, reversing lights, reclining front seats, front door armrests and door bins, split folding rear seat, carpeted glove box, grab handles, coat hooks, and vanity mirror on passenger sun visor. HLE, in addition to L features, had halogen headlights incorporating sidelights and indicators, side rubbing strip, clock, radio, and no rear mudflaps. S model, in addition to HLE features, had tinted glass, special seat trim, tachometer (revolution counter), digital clock, brake servo, and twin two-colour stripes replaced the side rubbing strip. The HLS re-instates the side rubbing strips and adds velour trimmed seats and door trim, front headrests, cloth faced sun visors, parcel shelf mat, carpeted boot, passenger door mirror, locking petrol flap, and more. Optional extras included interior light delay, additional front lights, electrically operated windows and door mirrors, radio/

stereo cassette unit, headlight washers. The halogen headlights with integrated sidelights and indicators that had been fitted to higher specification models from the start in 1980 were fitted to the 1985 model year L models and City and City X models for 1990. Also for 1985, the L models and above had a split fold rear seat and locking fuel flap; the City X had heated rear window, rear wash wipe and passenger door mirror; the HLE models received intermittent variable wipe for windscreen wipers; and all models received a larger 7.8 gallon fuel tank. For 1987, all models had reclining front seats, front door bins, reversing lights, and servo assisted brakes; L models got radio/stereo cassette units, and there were revisions to the model range which now consisted of City, City X, 1.0 L, 1.3 L, 1.3 GS, Sport, GTa, Studio 2, MG 1300 and MG Turbo. For 1990, the new Rover range of Metro models were Clubman 1.0, Clubman L, GS 1.3, GTa 1.3, and special

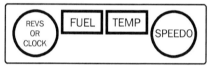

Instrument layout. 1980 HLS with tachometer, or 1982 HL with clock.

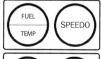

Instrument layout for 1985 Metro. Note: the HLE had a clock in the overhead console. Bottom, layout for 1988 GLS.

Note the position of fuel filler on these three-door cars. Early model on left, later model on right.

models Advantage and Knightsbridge. The Rover Metro range for 1994 was 1.1C, 1.1L, 1.1S, 1.4Si, 1.4 GTi, 1.4GSi, 1.4CD diesel, 1.4LD diesel with all models having a five-speed gear box, radio/cassette unit, rear screen wash wipe, driver and passenger door mirrors (body coloured on all models except C and CD), locking petrol cap and anti-theft alarm system, the front and rear suspension was now interconnected, and the heater and ventilation system had a three-speed fan. In addition to the above, intermittent wipe windscreen wipers were standard equipment on all except the C and CD models, and the S, Si, GTi and GSi had a tilting/removable glass sunroof.

COLOURS (1980): Ermine white, Applejack green, Nautilus blue, Vermilion red, Emberglow, Champagne beige, Snapdragon yellow, and Black. Metallics were Sombrero, Silver Birch, Peat, and Denim blue.
COLOURS (1990): Midnight blue, and

Cranberry red. Metallics were Quicksilver, Storm grey, Nordic, Amethyst, and Pearlescent Cherry red.

1982/83 specification

ENGINE: Four-cylinder, OHV. 1.0 model: bore 64.58mm, stroke 76.20mm, 998cc (60.89in³), maximum bhp 47 at 5500rpm, SU HIF38 carburettor. 1.3 model: bore 70.61mm, stroke 81.28mm, 1275cc (77.82in³), maximum bhp 60 at 5250rpm, SU HIF44 carburettor.
GEARBOX: Four-speed, floor-mounted gear change, synchromesh on all gears, 1.0 and 1.0 L models, ratios: top 3.647, 3rd 5.197, 2nd 7.965, 1st 13.30, reverse 13.37. All other models, ratios: top 3.44, 3rd 4.902, 2nd 6.55, 1st 12.546, reverse 12.611, with optional automatic, top 2.76, 3rd 4.03, 2nd 5.09, 1st 7.42. Front-wheel drive, final drive with helical spur gears, ratio 1.0 and 1.0 L models 3.647:1, 1.0 HLE 3.44:1, and all 1.3 models 3.44:1, automatic 2.76:1.
BRAKES: Dual circuit, front 8.38-inch discs, rear 7-inch drums, handbrake between front seats.
STEERING: Rack and pinion.
TYRES: 1.0 models 135 x 12, 1.3 models 155/70 x 12.
SUSPENSION: Front independent unequal length upper and lower arms, anti-roll bar, hydraulic shock absorbers, rear independent trailing radius arms, coil springs, Hydragas displacers front and rear.
DIMENSIONS: Length 11ft 2in (3.4m), width 5ft 0.9in (1.54m), height 4ft 4.3in (1.33m), wheelbase 7ft 4.6in (2.25m), track front 4ft 2.1in (1.27m), rear 4ft 2.2in (1.275m), turning circle 33ft 6in (10.2m), weight 15cwt 15lb (769kg) to 16cwt 3lb (815kg) according to model.
CAPACITIES: Fuel 6.5 gallons (29.5 litres), later models 7.8 gallons (34.5 litres). Boot 7.47ft³ (0.212m³) or 45.68ft³ (1.3m³) with rear seat folded down.

1994 specification

ENGINE: Four-cylinder, OHC. 1.1 model: bore 75mm, stroke 63mm, 1120cc (68.32in³), maximum 60PS, KIF carburettor. 1.4 Si: GSi, bore 75mm, stroke 79mm, 1396cc (85.16in³), maximum 75PS, single point fuel-injection. 1.4 GTi: four-cylinder, double OHC (16

Rear lights. Left: Early model. Right: Later model.

Gear change diagrams. Left, four-speed. Right, five-speed

valve), bore 75mm, stroke 79mm, 1396cc (85.16in³), maximum 103PS with multi point fuel-injection. CD and LD: four-cylinder, OHV, 1360cc (82.9in³) Peugeot/Rover diesel with indirect fuel-injection.

Austin Maestro

Introduced in 1983, and replacing both the Allegro and Maxi, this was another car from the drawing office of David Bache, with other designers – notably, Ian Beech – providing most of the input. Bache's earlier car, the Metro, had been produced largely by Harris Mann. The Maestro was only available as a five-door hatchback or two-door van. Those wanting a four-door car or an estate would have to wait another year until the launch of the Montego. MG variants of the Maestro appeared in 1983, and disappeared in 1991. The Austin version, however, was continued until 1995, by which time it had become part of the Rover car range, although it never wore the Rover name badge. The engines available were the 1275cc A-series and a 1600cc version of the E-series, which had been used in 1500cc and 1750cc form in the Allegro and Maxi. However, gone was the gearbox in sump arrangement of all the earlier front-wheel drive BMC cars; it was replaced by a Volkswagen-derived gearbox bolted onto the end of the engine. Also gone was the Hydragas suspension, replaced by a more conventional and popular MacPherson strut front suspension, with torsion beam style rear suspension. The Maestro highlighted many new features for Austin cars, including a bonded laminated front windscreen,

homofocal headlights, electronic engine management system, height adjustable front seatbelt anchorages, and more.

A new 1600cc engine, the 'S-series,' with electronic ignition, arrived in 1984. Also during 1984 were equipment upgrades, and additional models fitting in between the L and HLE were added to the range.

Further changes made during its lifetime included the introduction of diesel engined models, and then, following the introduction of the Rover 200, the whole range was revised and reduced. The original range consisted of Austin 1.3, 1.3L, 1.6L, 1.3HLE, 1.6HLS, MG 1600 and Vanden Plas.

Number produced: 605,411

Prices when introduced: 1.3 £4749, 1.6L £5499, 1.6 automatic £6290

Standard equipment at launch for the 1.3 model included water temperature gauge, trip

mileage recorder, heater and five adjustable air vents with three-speed fan, two-speed wipers with flick wipe, front windscreen washers, driver's sun visor with ticket pocket, two front parcel shelves, folding rear seat, anti-dazzle interior mirror, driver's door mirror, heated rear window, height adjustable inertia reel front seatbelts, reversing lights, rear foglights, hazard warning lights, front wheelarch liners, and more. 1.3L also had a radio, intermittent wipe front wipers, passenger glove box, centre console, reclining front seats, front headrests, front door bins and armrests, trimmed interior pillars, moulded rear parcel shelf, split fold rear seats, carpeted boot, and moulded plastic front and rear body coloured bumpers instead of bolt on steel bumpers painted black. The 1.6L was as the 1.3L, plus rear wash/wipe. 1.3HLE, in addition to 1.3L features, had an economy gauge, clock, internal adjustment of driver's door mirror, illuminated front ashtray in centre console, passenger grab handles, soft feel steering wheel, raised pile carpet, fabric trimmed rear parcel shelf, additional sound insulation, rear wash/wipe, strakes at each side of rear window, bright finish door handles, and locking fuel filler flap. 1.6HLS, in addition to 1.6L features, had a tachometer (revolution counter), clock, internal adjustment of driver's door mirror, passenger grab handles, soft feel steering wheel, raised pile carpet, fabric trimmed rear parcel shelf, additional sound insulation, bright finish door handles, and locking fuel filler flap. Optional extras (not available on all models) included, radio/stereo cassette unit, tilt/slide sunroof, electric front windows, central door locking, and automatic transmission (with a 1.6-litre engine). The 1987 range of Austin Maestro's consisted of City, City X, 1.3L, 1.6L, 1.6 automatic, 1.3 Mayfair, and 1.6 Mayfair. There was also a Vanden Plas 1.6, and an MG model now fitted with a 2.0-litre fuel injected engine instead of the original 1.6-litre. Standard equipment for the 1990 Clubman model, in addition to the equipment listed for the 1983 1.3 it replaced as the entry level model, included a clock, radio/stereo cassette unit, reclining front seats with headrests, front door bins, split folding rear seat, passenger door mirror, tilt/slide sunroof, rear window wash/wipe, decorative side trim and more. It did, however, retain

Instrument layout for L and HLE models.

Lower specification car with metal bumpers.

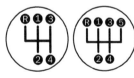

Gear change diagrams. Left: Four-speed. Right: Five-speed.

the black bolt on front and rear bumpers. Optional extras included a five-speed gearbox or automatic transmission (with a 1.6-litre engine).

COLOURS (1983/1985): Arum white, Rattan beige[1], Monza red[1], Champagne beige[2], Targa red[2], Clove brown, Eclipse blue, and Black.

Metallics were Silver leaf, Cashmere gold, Oporto red, Opaline green, Zircon blue, and Moonraker blue. ([1]1983 only, [2]1985 only.)

COLOURS (1990): White diamond, Oyster beige, Henley blue, Flame red, and Black. Metallics were Pulsar silver, Steel grey, Stone grey, Lynx bronze, British Racing green, Azure blue, Atlantic blue, and Pearlescent Cherry red.

1983 specification

ENGINE: Four-cylinder. 1.3 and 1.3L models: OHV, bore 70.61mm, stroke 81.28mm, 1275cc (77.82in[3]), maximum bhp 68 at 5800rpm, automatic choke SU HIF44 carburettor. 1.3HLE: as 1.3L except bhp 64 at 5500rpm. 1.6L and 1.6HLS: OHC, bore 76.2mm, stroke 87.6mm, 1598cc (97.48in[3]), maximum bhp 81 at 5500rpm, SU HIF44 carburettor.

GEARBOX: Four-speed, floor-mounted gear change, synchromesh on all gears. 1.3 and 1.3L ratios: top 3.79, 3rd 5.379, 2nd 8.09, 1st 13.387, reverse 13.219. 1.3HLE: top 2.723, 3rd 4.085, 2nd 5.835, 1st 13.42, reverse 12.33. 1.6L: top 3.54, 3rd 5.02, 2nd 7.547, 1st 13.42, reverse 12.33. 1.6HLS: five-speed, synchromesh on all gears, ratios: top 2.762, 4th 3.54, 3rd 5.02, 2nd 7.547, 1st 13.42, reverse 12.33. Front-wheel drive, final drive with helical spur gears, ratios 1.3, 1.3L models: 4.17:1; 1.3HLE, 1.6L, 1.6HLS models: 3.89:1.

BRAKES: Dual circuit, power assisted, front 9.5-inch discs, rear 8-inch drums.

STEERING: Rack and pinion, collapsible steering column (in event of accident).

TYRES: 1.3 and 1.3L: 145 x 13, 1.3 HLE: 155 x 13, 1.6L and 1.6HLS: 165 x 13.

SUSPENSION: All models, front MacPherson strut with co-axle coil springs and telescopic shock absorbers, rear independent trailing arms with co-axle coil springs/telescopic shock absorbers and 'H' beam interconnection. In addition to the above, the 1.6 models have a front anti-roll bar.

DIMENSIONS: Length 13ft 3.5in (4.049m), width 4ft 8.7in (1.439m), height 4ft 8in (1.439m), wheelbase 8ft 2.7in (2.507m), track front 4ft 9.7in (1.465m), rear 4ft 8.7in (1.439m), ground clearance 5.5in (139cm), turning circle 33ft 10in (10.31m), weight – 1.3: 17cwt 25lb (875kg); 1.3L: 17cwt 3qtr 7lb (905kg); 1.3HLE: 18cwt 1lb (915kg); 1.6L: 18cwt 2qtr 11lb (945kg); 1.6HLS: 18cwt 3qtr 16lb (960kg).

CAPACITIES: Fuel 11.75 gallons (53 litres). Boot with rear seat folded down, 50ft[3] (1.42m[3]).

1990 specification

ENGINE: Petrol S-series, four-cylinder, OHC, bore 76.2mm, stroke 87.58mm, 1598cc (97.48in[3]), SU HIF44E carburettor. Diesel, four-cylinder, OHC, bore 84.5mm, stroke 89mm, 1994cc (121.63in[3]), Bosch EVPE fuel-injection.

Austin Montego

Introduced in 1984, this replaced the Austin Ambassador and Morris Ital (formerly Marina). No Morris cars were produced after 1983. The Montego was almost a four-door version of the Maestro, sharing its doors and floorpan, but no other body panels. A new estate came, a few months after the saloon, replacing the Ital estate, and providing an option for those who wanted more load space than the hatchback Maestro could offer. Changes to the original styling were made by Roy Axe, who had worked for Rootes and Chrysler. Introduced a year after the Maestro, the Montego had the S-series 1.6 engine from the start, instead of the R-series that had been derived from the Allegro and Maxi. It also had a sturdier dashboard, but retained the proven A-series 1.3 engine, which had been around for decades, for its entry level models. The 2.0-litre O-series engine was from the Ambassador. The full range was the 1.3, 1.6, 1.6L, 1.6HL, 2.0HL, 2.0HLS saloons, 1.6, 1.6L, 1.6HL, 2.0HL, 2.0HLS estates, Vanden Plas 2.0 and MG 2.0EFI saloons, and a Vanden Plas estate introduced in 1985. Like the Maestro, the Austin name was dropped during the late 1980s, and there were changes made to the range and equipment levels throughout its life until it was discontinued in 1994. The estates continued in production a few months longer than the saloons.

Number produced: 571,640 all models.
Price when introduced: Saloons: 1.3 £5281, 1.6L £6159, 2.0HL £7195. Estates: 1.6L £6970, 2.0HL £8125.
Standard equipment at launch for the 1.3 and 1.6 models included water temperature gauge, trip mileage recorder, radio, heating/ventilation with three-speed fan, two-speed wipers with flick wipe, front windscreen washers, driver's sun visor, passenger sun visor with vanity mirror, one piece moulded facia, lockable glove box, driver's door bin, reclining front seats with adjustable headrests, adjustable front seatbelt anchorage points, heated rear window, interior bonnet and boot release, lockable fuel flap, driver and passenger door mirrors, halogen headlights, reversing lights, rear foglights and moulded plastic body-coloured bumpers. 1.6L added a clock, radio/stereo cassette unit, additional warning lights, passenger door bin, oddments trays by front seats, cassette storage box, internally adjustable door mirrors, side rubbing strip,

courtesy light in boot, and a five-speed gearbox. 1.6HL and 2.0HL added variable delay intermittent wipe windscreen wipers, tachometer, upholstered front and rear headrests, split folding rear seat with a centre armrest, cut pile carpet, and tinted glass. 2.0HL also had ventilated front disc brakes, while 2.0HLS added electric front windows, central door locking, and remote release fuel flap. Optional extras (not available on all models) included sliding steel sunroof, headlight washers, automatic transmission, power-assisted steering,

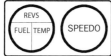

Instrument layout for the HL and HLS.

rear seatbelts, and more. The 1988 range consisted of 1.6, 1.6L, 2.0L, 2.0DL, 1.6SL, 2.0SL, 2.0DSL, 2.0GTi, 2.0GSi saloons and estates. The basic 1.6 model gained a radio/stereo cassette unit, internally adjustable door mirrors, and side rubbing strips. The 1.6L and new 2.0L models had adjustable lumbar support for the front seats, glass sunroof, rear headrests, and more. Two-tone paint was a free option on all saloons from L models upwards, and all 1.6 models now had a five-speed gearbox. The 1992 range included petrol engine saloons: 1.6 Clubman, 1.6LX, 2.0LXi, 2.0SLXi; diesel engine saloons: 2.0D Clubman, 2.0DLX, 2.0DSLX; petrol engine estates: 1.6 Clubman, 1.6LX, 2.0LXi, 2.0SLXi, 2.0i Countryman; and diesel engine estates: 2.0D Clubman, 2.0DLX, 2.0DSLX, 2.0 Countryman. All 2.0-litre engines came with fuel-injection and catalytic converters, and all models had rear seatbelts, an electric tilt and slide sunroof (manually operated on Clubman models). Lumbar adjustment for the driver's seat, and electric front windows and tinted glass were standard on all models except Clubman, all estates had an integrated roof rack, and the Countryman estate had an extra row of seats incorporating headrests and seatbelts; they were rearward facing and folded into the load compartment floor when not in use.

COLOURS (1985): Arum white, Champagne beige, Targa red, Clove brown, Eclipse blue, and Black. The metallics were Silver leaf,

Cashmere gold, Oporto red, Opaline green, Zircon blue, and Moonraker blue.

COLOURS (1990): White diamond, Oyster beige, Henley blue, Flame red, and Black. Metallics were Pulsar silver, Steel grey, Stone grey, Lynx bronze, British racing green, Azure blue, Atlantic blue, and Pearlescent Cherry red.

COLOURS (1992): White diamond, Midnight blue*, Henley blue, Flame red, and Black. Metallics were Quicksilver*, British racing green, Nordic blue*, Pearlescent Caribbean blue*, Pearlescent Nightfire red*. LX and SLX saloons were available with a two-tone paint finish, the lower half in Tempest grey. (*Not available on Clubman models).

1985 specification

ENGINE: 1.3 model: four-cylinder, OHV, bore 70.61mm, stroke 81.28mm, 1275cc ($77.82in^3$), maximum bhp 67 at 5600rpm, SU HIF44 carburettor. 1.6 models: four-cylinder, OHC, bore 76.2mm, stroke 87.6mm, 1598cc ($97.48in^3$), maximum bhp 83 at 5600rpm, SU HIF44E carburettor. 2.0 models: four-cylinder, OHC, bore 84.45mm, stroke 89mm, 1994cc ($121.63in^3$), maximum bhp 102 at 5500rpm, SU HIF44E carburettor.

GEARBOX: Four-speed, floor-mounted gear change, synchromesh on all gears. 1.3 ratios: top 3.863, 3rd 5.466, 2nd 8.263, 1st 14.684, reverse 13.473. Five-speed, synchromesh on all gears. 1.6L, 1.6HL ratios: top 2.802, 4th 3.582, 3rd 5.068, 2nd 7.66, 1st 13.616, reverse 12.493. Five-speed

(Honda derived), synchromesh on all gears. 2.0HL, 2.0HLS ratios: top, 2.52, 4th 3.339, 3rd 4.496, 2nd 6.89, 1st 11.508, reverse 11.811. Front-wheel drive, final drive with helical spur gears. Ratios: 1.3 model 4.25:1, 1.6 models 3.941:1, 2.0 models 3.937:1.

BRAKES: Dual circuit, power assisted, front 9.5-inch discs, rear 8-inch drums.

STEERING: Rack and pinion, collapsible steering column (in event of accident).

TYRES: 1.3 and 1.6: 165SR x 13. 1.6L, 1.6HL, 2.0HL, 2.0HLS: 180/65 x 14 TD.

SUSPENSION: All models: front MacPherson strut with co-axle coil springs and telescopic shock absorbers, rear independent trailing arms with co-axle coil springs/telescopic shock absorbers and 'H' beam interconnection. In addition to the above, the 1.6 models have a front anti-roll bar. Note: some estates have self-levelling rear suspension.

DIMENSIONS: Length saloons, 14ft 7.8in (4.46m), estate 14ft 7.9in (4.468m), width 5ft

Model with Rover badge on boot, and later 'flat' rear lights; early cars had 'ribbed' units.

7.3in (1.7m), height saloon 4ft 7.9in (1.42m), estate 4ft 9in (1.447m), wheelbase 8ft 5.2in (2.57m), track front 4ft 9.68in (1.465m), rear 4ft 8.69in (1.44m), ground clearance 6in (15.5cm), turning circle 35ft 4in (10.46m), weight, saloons 1.3 18cwt 2qtr 23lb (950kg), 1.6HL 19cwt 2qtr 10lb (995kg), 2.0HLS 1 ton 1qtr 3lb (1030kg), estates 1.6 1 ton 3qtr 24lb (1065kg), 2.0L 1 ton 1cwt 3qtr 22lb (1115kg).

CAPACITIES: Fuel 11 gallons (50 litres), Boot – saloon: 18.4ft³ (0.52m³) with 1.7ft³ under boot mat, or 26.9ft³ (0.76m³) with rear seat folded down. Estate: 15.2ft³ (0.43m³) or 57.2ft³ (1.62m³) with seats folded down.

1990 specification

ENGINE: 1.6 and 2.0 petrol models as 1985 model year, except maximum power marginally increased following introduction of electronic carburettor control. The 2.0GTi and 2.0GSi, introduced in 1988, have Bosch fuel-injection, instead of the SU carburettor fitted to other 2.0 models. Diesel models, four-cylinder, OHC, bore 84.5mm, stroke 89mm, 1994cc, (121.63in³), maximum bhp 81 at 4500rpm, Bosch EPVE fuel-injection and Garrett T2 turbocharger.

GEARBOX: Five-speed, floor-mounted gear change, synchromesh on all gears. 1.6 models, ratios: top 2.999, 4th 3.805, 3rd 5.132, 2nd 7.954, 1st 13.65, reverse 13.02. 2.0 models, ratios: top 2.551, 4th 3.339, 3rd 4.409, 2nd 6.89, 1st 11.508, reverse 12.20, optional automatic with four-speed gearbox. 2.0 engine, ratios: top 2.71, 3rd 4.034, 2nd 5.02, 1st 8.845, reverse 10.37. Diesel models, ratios:

top 2.363, 4th 3.093, 3rd 4.457, 2nd 6.718, 1st 11.546, reverse 11.306. Front-wheel drive, final drive with helical spur gears, ratios: 1.6 models 4.2:1, 2.0 petrol models 3.937:1, automatic 3.667:1, diesel 3.647:1.

Left: Early style front. Right: Later style front.

Gear change diagrams. Left: Four-speed. Right: Five-speed

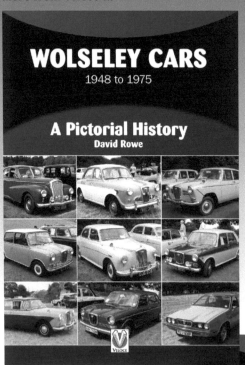
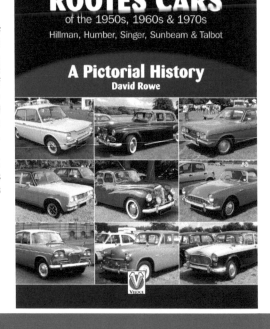

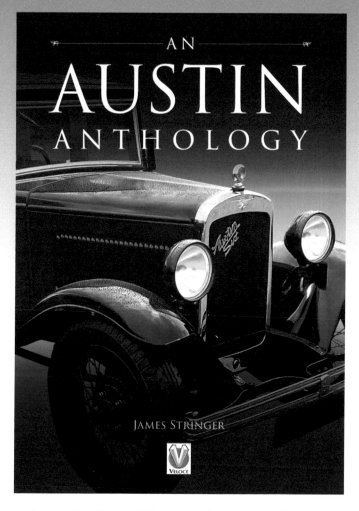

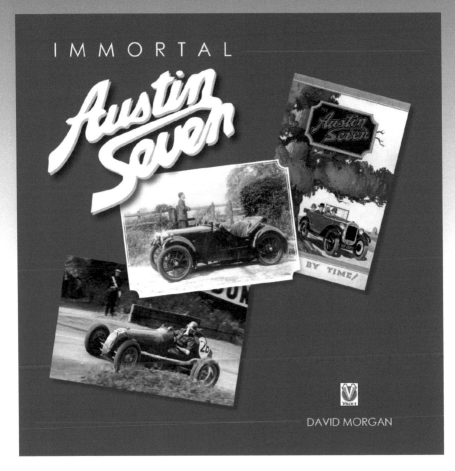

Immortal Austin Seven tells the story of this most popular of prewar cars in all its variations, from the earliest Chummy of the 1920s through Sports, Military, Box and Ruby Saloons to the exquisite Twin Cam racers of the late 1930s. The book includes period, detail drawings and rarely seen photographs – a must for the Austin Seven enthusiast.

ISBN: 978-1-845849-79-5
Hardback • 24.8x24.8cm • 228 pages • 319 colour and b&w pictures